Wishing you joy

Billie Hughes Locke

MORE THAN ONE

ANGEL

MORE THAN ONE ANGEL

BILLIE HUGHES LOCKE

WINEPRESS WP PUBLISHING

Printed in the United States of America

Packaged by WinePress Publishing, PO Box 428, Enumclaw, WA 98022. The views expressed or implied in this work do not necessarily reflect those of WinePress Publishing. Ultimate design, content, and editorial accuracy of this work are the responsibilities of the author.

The angel cover girl is the author's granddaughter. Sara Elizabeth Tolson recently celebrated her sixth birthday. Her hobbies include swimming, singing, gardening, art, and reading. She attends modeling classes and homeschool. Sara lives with her parents, Ed and Kathie, and her younger brother, Wesley Aaron.

Unless otherwise noted, all scriptures are taken from the King James Version of the Holy Bible.

ISBN 1-57921-244-1
Library of Congress Catalog Card Number: 99-64804

This book is dedicated to my children.
Your lives came through me. A reason to live was born in me
through each of you.

Contents

Acknowledgements

A special thank you to my angel sister Diane
who brings healing in her wings.

Introduction

There is no way around it: I was a difficult child.

My parents didn't have a fancy name like "middle child syndrome" to blame for the behavior of their impossible offspring. The word *syndrome* alone would have made them feel better. But fifty years ago, there was no such terminology. Their best explanation was that I was maladjusted.

However, that suggested someone hadn't adjusted me properly, so what had they done wrong? Their firstborn, Diane, was a saint, so they couldn't blame my difficulties on genetics. Besides comparing me to Diane, Daddy often wondered aloud if I was a judgment, or maybe possessed.

After Diane, a second child was born to Lawrence and Alice Place Hughes before I poked my head into this world. Little Larry, named for Daddy, died from complications of pneumonia at only six months old. When Mama and Daddy found out a third baby was on the way, they lit candles and prayed for a son to take their Larry's place.

Well, on June 15, 1942, I rocked their boat, which may have been an omen. They had chosen only one name. And since I was clearly not a boy, they couldn't, just couldn't call me William. How it would have shocked people to hear them introduce me, "This is our daughter, William." So, they decided to call me Billie.

Later I wondered why I had a boy's name. When I finally learned that my birth certificate says my name is Billie and the church baptismal record gives it as Wilhelmenia, I said, "No wonder I've been so messed up! Nobody knew who I was! How could they expect me to know how to act?"

Although I really tried to be good, I didn't have whatever it takes to be saintly, like my older sister Diane. What I had was a knack for causing people to question the existence of God. You might ask what child's behavior could cause such a reaction in adults? Unless you have a child who defies all reason, it's hard to understand.

For parents entrusted with a child showing middle child syndrome (MCS), it will be comforting to know there is hope. The pages that follow may also offer hope for anyone who has suffered neglect as a child, abuse as a wife, or pain from their own rebellious choices in life. God is so wonderful! He meant everything I experienced in life, including the poverty and despair—all of it—for good.

Section I.
Middle Child

Me at nineteen.

CHAPTER 1

Why Can't You Be Like Diane?

Every time I did something outlandish, poor Daddy shook his head and said, "Dear God, why can't you be like your sister Diane? Watch Diane and you will learn something!"

I watched and I saw my older sister washing clothes, scrubbing floors, and preparing meals. All I saw was that Diane worked too hard. What a drag! I must admit that once in a while I wanted the praise Diane earned. But it seemed to me there was more fun in getting attention through shock. Then the same parents who gazed adoringly at Diane looked at me as if they were examining a species from another planet.

Even when Mama rocked me and sang, I wondered if she was thinking about her little baby Larry in heaven. I loved putting my head against her chest and feeling the sound of her voice, singing a song about a little girl. At least she knew I was a female! I was very sorry about what happened to her baby Larry; however, it was my turn. I was glad that I, not some boy named Little William, was on Mama's lap.

Things started to change when the house filled up with other kids. First there was Joe, born when I was three. Then Kathleen arrived when I was five. More and more, Mama avoided us. It's a wonder I ever spoke to her after I discovered her cunning methods of getting rid of me for the day. There was, what I called, her nine-penny trick. She told us that there were ten pennies outside, but the tenth was never there to begin with. Mama also said if I got close enough to a bird to sprinkle salt on its tail, I could tame it and make it my pet. I spent many hours lurking about the yard with a stupid bag of salt. When I figured out there was no way I could get sufficiently close to a bird without scaring it off, I imagined Mama looking out the window and laughing. I admit my Irish eyes saw red.

Our family lived in Philadelphia until I was six, when Daddy left the military. He moved us to Norfolk, Virginia, my mother's hometown, where he was able to get a good civil service job. That trip to Norfolk in our loaded Jeep seemed to take forever. My sitting/sleeping space was at one side of the back, on the floorboard. It was cramped but warm.

Shortly after we arrived at my grandparents' house on Chesapeake Street, Grandmama turned on their radio. We couldn't believe our ears! A lady's voice welcomed Alice and Lawrence, Diane, Billie, Joe, and Kathleen. Mama said, "That's your Aunt Edna, my oldest sister. She has her own radio program with Uncle Eddie Pifer. She sings and he plays the guitar. She's letting the whole world know we are in town!"

We children felt like celebrities for the longest time.

I loved Grandmama and Granddaddy and their home. Everything about that old brown house was beautiful to me. On the first floor were two bedrooms. They slept in the front one. Mama and Daddy took over Mama's little brother Jimmy's room. In between the bedrooms was a bathroom and another door, which revealed the tiniest attic stairs.

My grandparents had finished off the attic, making one very large space with low ceilings at the sides and containing storage compartments. We children slept in that cozy room. It was a magical place when nobody else was there. I could be anyone I chose to be, like royalty in a castle or a New York City resident in its tallest skyscraper.

It was fine except for Jimmy. Because he was younger, I could not and would not call him "uncle." Furthermore, I thought he was one weird kid. At dinner he never ate what everybody else was eating. He wanted plain spaghetti with tomato sauce poured right out of the can. I guess my Grandmama was tired by the time he came along because she regularly gave in to him to keep peace.

Mama nearly had a heart attack when Jimmy cut off Joe's finger with a lawn mower. Jimmy said it was an accident. Joe said that Jimmy pointed to a rock and told him to pull it out. When Joe reached for the rock, Jimmy pushed the mower, and my little brother permanently lost the top of his middle finger, down to the first joint.

Mama's other sister in Norfolk, Aunt Ruthie, also lived close to my grandparents in the cutest little Quonset hut in Ocean View. In the early years, we saw more of her than the rest of Mama's family. Like her sisters, she had married young, but she had gotten the prize. She and Uncle Lloyd Wilson had one child, David. Aunt Ruthie Wilson loved that kid to pieces.

My daddy said Aunt Ruthie could cheer up a brick wall. She had the biggest, softest heart of all. People felt good to be in the same room with her. The thing I liked best was the way she held my face in her hands, looked directly in my eyes, and told me she loved me. Those warm eyes sent her words deep inside my heart, making them stick where nobody could ever take them away.

Uncle Lloyd was a good house builder, so he furnished the house plans for ours. He, Daddy, Uncle Eddie, and anyone else who could swing a hammer worked hard building the front part of our new home. To us, it was the best home in the world. We didn't mind that we wore one another's clothes and made do with very little. We used our imaginations and depended on each other. Life was good. Watching Daddy build was a great experience in which we were all part of the grand design. He kept his saws in our bedroom until we had a garage. We walked on concrete floors and slept on horsehair mattresses but it was all right; we were heading toward something better.

Mama told great stories of her childhood. The best tale of all was Mama and Aunt Edna's venture into the home fuel-supply business:

"One day we had to pee real bad and ducked into an old shed. After we peed in a jar, we saw some kerosene lamps and noticed that our pee was the same color as the kerosene. We were struck with a brilliant scheme that was sure to make money. We poured some of our pee into an empty oil lamp. Slippin' into the house, we helped ourselves to matches. Then we went back to the shed and fired up the lamp. To our amazement, it lit up!

"We never stopped to consider that there might be some kerosene left on the wick. Oh no. We thought we had some really powerful pee there, so we drank gallons of water to make more. Then we poured it into jars and sold it to the neighbors. We even demonstrated how nicely it burned.

"We got in big trouble when our customers came knockin' at Grandmama's door. They were hootin' mad and callin' us a couple of thievin', up-to-no-good delinquents."

Mama always had stories. Her childhood nickname was Bumps. An adventurous but ungraceful kid, she fell a lot. She also ate glass. Aunt Edna, who always tried to outdo everybody, ate dirt. Mama said it was no contest—she was the all-time champion of clever stunts:

"I claimed I had seen a real fire engine and said I could get one to come to my house. To prove it, I set a tree on fire in the front yard. When the blaze got goin' good, Grandmama came runnin' across the field carryin' grocery bags in her arms. She was screamin' and yellin', 'Alice! Alice!' She was so mad she could've chewed a rope in half.

"I don't know how Grandmama knew who was behind my stunt, but she did. I was in trouble for a long time. I didn't care one bit, though, because in no time at all there was a big red fire engine sittin' right in the front yard. People came from everywhere just to get a look."

I was convinced Mama was the top kid who ever lived on that street.

Those stories made life more tolerable than it might have been while I was growing up on Lesner Avenue. Most of the homes were built during the Second World War for military families, all middle class, except for the people who lived in the junkyard at the end of the block. Come to find out, the man who owned it, Mr. Akers, had more money than the rest of us. He just liked living with wrecked cars and parts of things lying around in his yard. He rented the several shacks on his property to people passing through.

Mr. Akers never wanted the neighborhood kids to hang around his property. My daddy didn't want us to hang around there either. But sometimes I'd sneak over to talk to Mr. Aker's daughter, Joyce. I figured Daddy didn't need to know everything. Joyce's brother, Robert, was incredibly good looking. Joyce was a sweet girl. She looked sad when she told me her mother was dead. I figured I was lucky, even though my mother was less and less at home.

When my parents were out working, which was most of the time, I could be found wandering the neighborhood. I discovered people were basically good, even though caught up in their own little productions. Thankfully, they opened their doors and welcomed me into their lives. In that special sense of community in those days, neighbors tried to look after small girls searching for love and acceptance.

After we moved in, Daddy built the rest of our house because it wasn't large enough. I was ten years old, and Mama was expecting another baby.

The night baby Alice was born at the hospital, Daddy came into the bedroom and sat on my bed. Crying, he said, "It's a girl, and she's beautiful."

"What's her name, Daddy?"

"Her full name is Alice Carol Hughes. Carol is for the Christmas songs this time of year. She has a head full of dark hair like mine." He smiled.

I preferred to see him smiling than crying. Later I would learn that Alice's birth date was the same day as Pearl Harbor Day, but I don't know why Daddy cried.

When they brought Alice home from the hospital, she was the prettiest baby I'd ever seen. Her skin was like fine porcelain; dark hair framed her face, making her look like an angel; her eyes were clear blue . . . but downcast, haunting. Sometimes in the middle of the night, I'd see her staring out at something. I wondered if she missed our mother.

Mama went to work very soon after Alice was born. Alice lay in her crib for hours, not making a sound or bothering anybody. Bottles filled with lumpy curds were left in the crib because no one thought to take them out. She didn't have many clothes, either. As she grew, her diapers hung down to her knees when they were full. I was glad when she learned to use the potty.

Before Mama went to work, she had time to take care of us and cook. I didn't understand then how my mother would want to leave us. I learned that it wasn't for the money; my father had a good civil service job. Mama just wanted to be free of taking care of her children. As a waitress, she apparently found some of that freedom. Some mothers never have a chance to grow up before they are saddled with too much responsibility.

If the residents on the street where I grew up were a lifeline, my relatives were beacons of light when the sky grew dark and threatening. Even Diane, as much as I hated being compared to her, gave me a sense of security our Mama was unable or unavailable to give. No matter what the big scene, relatives and neighbors made up an unforgettable cast of characters in my unfolding life.

Those among my father's family in West Virginia, for instance . . .

CHAPTER 2

. . . .

Summer Picnics
and Mischief

S ummer vacation in West Virginia with Daddy's family was something we kids looked forward to all year. Daddy left us there because his vacation time was not as long as ours was. His father, my
Grandpa Hughes, died when I was six months old, and my grandmother,
who wanted to be called "Mom," never remarried. She had a boyfriend
named Elmo, who was a very nice man. He had strange patches on his
bald head that he called liver spots. Daddy and his brother, Owen, told
their mom they would be upset if she even thought about marrying
him. Elmo was not a Catholic.

Mom Hughes was always on the go. She made her mark on the community as the first president of the VFW ladies' auxiliary. Her picture
still hangs in the VFW lodge and town hall. Mom liked to put up her
specialty, chili, in jars and count them to compare how many she made
from year to year. She also canned applesauce, beans, and pickles.

She had the only outhouse I was ever in. I didn't like it too much
because cows roamed around in the field nearby. We had to be really
careful just before dark.

Mom's bedroom was a loft that could be reached only by a flight of
narrow stairs. In the loft was her jewelry box. She had the biggest ears

I ever saw and didn't mind wearing huge earrings to show them off. When she walked briskly, those ears swayed back and forth so much it's a wonder she didn't get a headache. When she was gone, I loved to try on her earbobs and stare at myself in her old dresser mirror. I wondered if my ears would ever lay flat, or would they keep getting bigger like my grandmother's.

In her desk, Mom stored stacks of greeting cards for every occasion. Saying it didn't cost much to send a kind word to someone who was sick or just needed cheering up, my grandmother wrote notes in every card she sent.

"It just plain makes folks feel better to know that someone cares about them," she'd say. For each of our birthdays, she sent two dollars inside one of her best cards.

Uncle Owen, a warm and gentle man and an engineer on the B&O Railroad, liked to keep a number of hunting dogs. He also had two housedogs, both basset hounds, both named Jasper. I don't know why; he just did. When one died, he'd get another and name him Jasper too.

At the gas station in Fort Ashby with Uncle Owen, people thought we were his kids. He smiled really big when folks said how much we favored him. Uncle Owen always wanted children of his own but never had any. Every year, I wished that he would adopt me, but I was afraid to ask.

Mama told me that he tried to adopt a little girl once, but his wife, Aunt Evelyn, became jealous, and they sent the girl back to the orphanage. Aunt Evelyn sucked on lemons to hide the smell of whiskey. She hid bottles of the stuff all over the house, even in her plants. But she was loads of fun and acted like a kid too. When it was my turn to stay with them, she took me out to lie on the side of a hill and eat green apples with salt while we picked out shapes of things in the clouds.

Aunt Genevieve, Daddy's only sister, and her husband, Uncle Les Hartman, were good to us. Their passion was the Pittsburgh Pirates baseball team. Listening to games on the radio, Aunt Genevieve said the rosary for them. If they won, she hollered, "Thank you, Jesus!" She prayed for the "Fighting Irish" football team too.

My father took that whole Irish thing very seriously. I never could figure out what was so Irish about any of the Notre Dame teams. They surely didn't look Irish, and they had some very strange names, nothing like Kelly, or Bailey, or Murphy.

Like Aunt Evelyn, Aunt Genevieve also hid whiskey around the house. According to Mama, when she thought nobody was looking, she took a swig. Still, Aunt Genevieve always tried to do special things for us when we visited her. Uncle Les liked to sneak up on me and say, "Boo!" But the most special thing was that Aunt Genevieve made sure we had plenty to eat every day.

The biggest event of each summer, the Firemen's Fourth of July Picnic, was held at campgrounds by Patterson's Creek. The adults called it Peterson's Crack, and they all grinned when they said it. If we said it, they did not grin.

For the picnic, the ladies' auxiliary of the VFW put frosty bottles of root beer in big tubs along with every other kind of soda pop. We ate hot dogs and hamburgers to our heart's content. I strolled up and down the campgrounds so every person could see me having a big time. After we ate all we could hold, we put on sneakers, climbed a rope, and pushed each other right into "Peterson's Crack." The bottom of the creek was covered with rocks and sharp pebbles. Our West Virginia cousins, Jimmy and Tootie, whose real name was Ruth, were used to the rocks. My feet got big blisters and stayed sore for weeks, but we had such fun, I didn't care.

After swimming all we wanted, we dried off and ate more hot dogs and hamburgers. I couldn't get enough of that delicious mountain root beer. That picnic was always the highlight of our summer.

Except one year, near the end of summer vacation, when I got into a whole lot of trouble with my girlfriend, Gloria Funk. She knew everybody in Fort Ashby, West Virginia, because her folks owned the combination grocery store/gas station. Gloria said she knew of a house where we could have a lovely afternoon. She claimed the sweet old lady who lived there was away and wouldn't mind at all. In fact, the dear soul would probably be happy somebody was checking on her house. We crawled in a window and had fun looking at everything.

When we got hungry, Gloria said she was a good cook. But the cupboards were bare; all we found was some flour. That lying Gloria said she had watched her mama make biscuits so many times she could do it with her eyes closed. So we mixed and we poured, and all we got were flat little things that felt like rubber and could take out our teeth.

Gloria's gravy looked like Phillips Milk of Magnesia and tasted even worse. We straightened up the house and went to the grocery store/gas station for some real food.

Soon after that day, my friend and I were in trouble. How had the adults put two and two together and placed us at the scene of the crime? I was convinced it was an eternal secret that only adults knew and refused to tell kids.

Next thing we knew, Gloria's aunt was yelling and pushing us right back to the old lady's house. We had to clean the mess that I thought we had already cleaned. When wet, everything had looked fine. But, when it dried, the flour was easy to spot, stuck like glue to the floor, table, counters, and stove. Gloria and I scrubbed and scrubbed all day until there wasn't a spot of dirt or flour on anything.

But were they satisfied? After all our hard work, Gloria and I had to apologize to the owner and wait until she said we could go. We thought it unreasonable, to say the least. For what seemed like an eternity, she said nothing. Finally, she nodded her head. Gloria's aunt told us to wait outside. We could sense the worst was yet to come.

Right in front of the population of Fort Ashby, Gloria's aunt took off her shoe and whipped us. She spanked our behinds with that monstrous clodhopper all the way home, and nobody did a thing to stop her. The rest of that summer vacation was ruined because people looked at us, shook their heads, and made *tut-tut* sounds but said nothing to us.

When Daddy came to take us home, I thought he would mete out the same punishment, only worse. Preparing myself for what could happen, I already knew what he'd say: "Dear God, why can't you be like your sister Diane? What have I done to deserve this? Billie, when are you going to learn to do something besides get into trouble? What, tell me, what am I going to do with you?"

I racked my brain trying to think up some humongous, believable lie to get me out of that kettle of fish. I decided to blame it all on Gloria.

From the moment he arrived, Daddy never saw a better Billie. Sweating bullets, I sweetly tried to butter him up, scared he wouldn't get over the humiliating episode his child had been involved in. After all, he was West Virginia's "Golden Boy," the one who had gotten out of that part of the country and had made them proud.

When he didn't say or do anything about my misadventure, I figured maybe he was saving it all up to eventually blow. I stayed on my best behavior. He never mentioned it.

Maybe no one told him about the miserable cooking caper. I certainly didn't. Or maybe, when he had learned about it, he decided to leave me hanging—afraid, at least temporarily, to misbehave.

CHAPTER 3

The Magic Attic

Back in Norfolk, I often walked the short distance to Grandmama's house, where we had initially stayed upon moving to town while Daddy built the first stage of our house. I wanted to play in her magic attic.

Grandmama's maiden name was Ruth Irma Harrell, and she was the great-granddaughter of a Cherokee Indian chief. Proud of her heritage, she showed me a picture of the chief dressed in full headdress, looking very handsome. She told me about her three siblings—an older sister, Eda, and two deceased brothers, James and Edward. The brothers worked as linemen for Virginia Electric and Power Company and died from electrical shock, in different years, each on his twenty-seventh birthday.

Looking like an Indian squaw, Grandmama stood four feet ten inches in her "stockinged feet," as she said. To me she seemed as round as she was tall, always dressed in brightly colored frocks enhanced by pins with sparkly, colored stones. Her dark hair hung in long curls, tied back with pretty ribbons and bows from her full face.

My grandfather's full name was Elias Arthur Place. Both Granddaddy and Grandmama liked flowers. Her favorites were peonies and pink roses. His was the pansy; he was forever amazed at how the blooms could stay alive in snow.

Inside their house, well stocked with kid treats, something good was always cooking on Grandmama's stove. She loved seafood, especially if she caught it herself. Her favorite was steamed crabs. When it came to dinner rolls, hers could win first prize. And folks always felt welcome in her home.

I loved to spend the night. Before bedtime, I took a bath in her huge porcelain tub that sat on lion's feet. The water came up to my neck. When it got cold, I could pull the stopper with one foot and let more hot water in with the other. Grandmama poured stuff into the bath that smelled like her and made the water soft. I'd sing every song I knew. Grandmama said my singing sounded great coming from the bathroom. When my fingers wrinkled, I knew it was time to get out.

Sometimes I slept in her attic. I relished the place. It had lots of nooks and crannies. In one corner was a trunk filled with her old clothes. I played dress-up, sometimes pretending to be a queen with adoring servants tending to my every whim. The best game was competing for the title of Miss America. I sang and danced and recited poetry. Grandmama said my routines were the best. The outcome was always the same: I'd accept my crown and stroll down the runway while Grandmama smiled and Bert Parks sang for the newly crowned Miss America.

When it was really cold outside, Grandmama let me sleep on the couch in the front room. When the trolley cars passed by out front, the whole house rattled.

I asked, "If I get on that trolley and stay on, where will it take me?"

"Biddy [her pet name for me], it's like anything in life. You can go anywhere you choose."

On the mantel of the front room, a sweet chiming clock comforted and lulled me to sleep.

Apple and pear trees grew in the backyard. All year long Grandmama saved brown bags to fill with fruit. She allowed Jimmy and me to earn spending money selling the fruit. Jimmy pulled the wagonload of fruit while I sat on the back. Grandmama said that if I ate the fruit and smacked my lips, everyone would want to buy some. It worked every time. We'd earn enough money to go to Ocean View Amusement Park. Back then a kid could go there and stay all day, and no one ever worried.

Grandmama's house became my refuge. When I was down, she knew. We'd climb into her big porch swing, then she'd wrap her gentle arms around me and sing. Her favorite gospel song still brings me courage and strength. If I close my eyes, I see her colorful dresses and sparkly pins in her dark hair.

> There is no pow'r can conquer you
> While God is on your side[1]

Granddaddy sensed when I was having trouble at home. He created funny stories to make me laugh and sang silly songs that made everybody smile. He'd dance around and shake his tail, and Grandmama would call him an old fool. Everybody liked his Joe Blow song: "Joe Blow from Idaho, got off the train and broke his toe. On the way back, he broke his back, sliding down the railroad track."

Granddaddy showed off their special painting and prized family heirloom. It hung for years above a sideboard in the dining room. He had done odd jobs during the Depression, and a lady who wanted a ditch dug, but who didn't have any money, paid him with the painting. She said he might be able to trade the painting of Mt. Vernon for cash. Because of its history and because it was uniquely painted on the backside of glass and set in a beautiful antique frame, my grandparents loved that painting and kept it.

My granddaddy knew hard times. Nothing had ever been a picnic for him, but he survived and kept his family fed. He didn't bellyache about hardships. Grandmama allowed that when he was a young man, he did go on the warpath a time or two.

All I saw was love in a Granddaddy who took joy from simple things. In his later years, he was thrilled when pop-top cans were invented. He spent hours in his backyard decorating a tree for Christmas with tabs from cans. Hooking them together, he made a garland and wrapped it around the tree.

Grandmama and Granddaddy were plain, ordinary people who, just like everyone, had their times of strength and weakness. They gave me something good to take on my journey. Their songs and laughter shrunk my problems, and they taught me to look for the silver lining. Grandmama often said, "Living can get the best of you if you let it." Maybe it was the Indian in her that imparted a wisdom all her own. Often she looked into my eyes and assured me that, no matter what happened, I was going to make it. "I can see that you will," she encouraged.

As I grew older and troubles deepened, I hoped she was right.

CHAPTER 4

My Sister, the Saint

Television was the grandest thing to ever hit Lesner Avenue. We had the first set in the neighborhood. It was so exciting! Everyone watched our test pattern through the windows. Among my favorite programs was *The Howdy Doody Show with Princess Summer Fall Winter Spring*, partly because of Granddaddy's tales about the Flathead Indians and partly because I loved her name. I fancied calling my first baby girl by that name.

After television, it wasn't so bad staying at home with just my siblings. Our fighting decreased. The selection of shows was so limited that we didn't argue about what to watch. Joe always wanted to see *Roy Rogers, King of the West*, which was fine with me because I loved Dale Evans, the queen of the West, and the theme song, "Happy Trails to You."

When Daddy was home, we had to watch boxing or *Victory at Sea*. The boxing matches weren't great, but watching Daddy was. We'd swear he was in the ring, with his fancy footwork and his *pow!* and *ugh!* sounds. Pretty soon he'd be telling us about his big fight with so-and-so.

Our local station had a show called *The Bob and Chauncey Show*, featuring a ventriloquist and his dummy. When I learned a portion of their program was devoted to local talent, I sparked a hot idea. Determined to hit it big and end up in Hollywood, I enlisted my girlfriend, Anita Durand. We chose to sing "It's Almost Tomorrow." Anita's father took us to the station for our debut. My daddy and Diane watched at home and reported that we were good, but there was no call from an agent.

School became a drag. Mostly I daydreamed. One of the nuns, I'll call her Sister Mary No Nonsense, should have been a baseball player. She threw erasers to wake me; they sailed across the room and hit me in the same spot every time. She did try to help me, though, with bags of used clothing. I wondered why nuns had to wear big bibs around their necks and fans on their heads. I once thought I'd be a nun to make Daddy proud, but I couldn't have hacked wearing the same drab thing every day. Besides, black was not my color.

Uncle Johnny, whose full name is John Arthur Place, had three children with his wife, Aunt Ann. Their names are Lawrence Arthur (he was named after my daddy because Uncle Johnny loved my father), Brenda, and Johnny Allen. Uncle Johnny's kids were always sweet and had nice things. As a young man, Uncle Johnny was a baker in the navy, and the family's house was full of good things to eat. Some things never change. Uncle Johnny's house is still full of goodies.

Aunt Nona married Ann's brother, whose name was Walter Brown McKee, and the children born to both families called themselves double cousins. Aunt Nona's children were Linda Lee, Michael Alex, and Jennette, the youngest, whom we called Jeanie. Aunt Nona's children were tender-hearted, giving, and I loved every minute that I spent with them when we were children.

Aunt Nona lived close to my school, Holy Trinity. When I didn't have bus money, I walked to visit her and my cousins. I enjoyed them all, then Aunt Nona would take me home. She had the sweetest smile and dimples. Her husband was a chief in the navy. Although his name was Walter, she called him Bill. Uncle Bill's sister, Ann, was married to my Uncle Johnny before she died of cancer. So the kids from both families really were double cousins, which I thought was pretty nifty.

I couldn't wait to play with my cousins, Linda, Michael, and Jennette, especially when my uncle was out to sea. Then Aunt Nona paid more attention to my cousins and me. When Uncle Bill was home, he tried to rule the roost, and we didn't have nearly as much fun.

Aunt Nona was a good cook, so I loved staying for dinner. When I griped about my home and how I wanted to grow up and get out of there, she just listened and told to tell me to stick it out, not run off and make a big mistake. Although I didn't always heed her advice, she never once said, "I told you so."

At home, I did so much I wasn't supposed to do. Most of the time I was grounded. When Daddy wasn't home, I simply went anywhere I wanted to go. His activities were easy enough to predict, and I knew when he would return. Our noisy stone driveway was helpful, too, in warning me of Daddy's approach. It gave me plenty of time to hang up the phone or hide something I didn't want him to see, like make-up.

I didn't get away with everything, though. At night, when girlfriends tapped on my window, I unscrewed the screen (with a screwdriver I kept hidden under my bed) and jumped out the window. We lay on the grass, puffed cigarettes, and told each other one big lie after another. One night, when I began feeling queasy, I crawled back inside. I replaced everything and got into bed for a nice snooze, thinking I had really pulled a fast one on old Dad.

Just then Daddy flashed on the light and said, "Goodnight, Eileen. I'm glad you enjoyed your little smoke."

I tiptoed around the house for a long time after, thinking he might blow his stack at any moment, but I guess he forgot. Maybe he was giving me the silent treatment to keep me on my toes.

I didn't know why I was a brat. Diane was everything good and worthy of praise. I just couldn't seem to be good, no matter how hard I tried. Sometimes I wondered if I had been adopted or accidentally switched at birth, but my little "daddy" hands and flat fingernails told me otherwise. Now I understand that I didn't have the proper spiritual training to overcome my rebellious nature.

Mary, the Holy Mother of God, was always busy listening to Diane so I prayed mostly to Jesus. When dark clouds loomed because of my behavior, I called upon St. Jude, promising "never again" and "if delivered, I will devote my remaining days to the needy." Still, I seemed to stay in trouble. What was wrong with me? Diane was truly sweet and kind. She even forgave me after I bit the finger off of her latex doll, stole her socks, and snooped in all her stuff.

Diane had a shrine to the Blessed Mother. She lit candles and placed wildflowers at Mary's feet. I was sure there was a stream of holy light from the statue going directly into my sister's head as she prayed. Maybe the rays came from Mary's fingertips, which reached out to Diane, kneeling for what seemed like hours. Mary's eyes were always looking down. I thought she was probably afraid I'd come along with an impossible request.

My sister's best friend in those days was Barbara Hall. She and Diane dressed alike: men's white shirts knotted in front and jeans rolled up to their knees. Diane had a peroxide streak in her hair and smoked Barbara's cigarettes.

Billy Nottingham was Diane's only boyfriend until she met Chuck Hughes, whom she later married. Chuck was better looking and had the same last name as ours. But Billy's parents owned property, which they called "the lot." He loved taking Diane there to show off, and he gave her his high school ring, which she wore on a chain around her neck. It must have been important to Billy because he often asked Diane to be careful and not chip the setting.

Barbara and Diane taught Alice her first words and laughed like crazy when she said "Nockernoodle [for Nottingham]," "to da lot," and "don' chip da ring." They had to take Alice with them everywhere or Diane couldn't go. Alice enjoyed going with them because she might get french fries or a sip of Pepsi.

When Diane was home and not studying or praying at her shrine, she was our mother, until she went away for nurse's training. She cooked for us and tried to buy enough food with the two dollars Mama sometimes left in the kitchen. We all liked the way she combined hamburger with tomato soup and poured the mix on mashed potatoes. She washed our clothes, tried to teach us manners, and generally took care of us.

Our mama wasn't much older than Diane. We didn't see Mama except after school as she got ready for work. Her make-up had to be just right because she worked in a fancy restaurant. Every night, she stayed late to prepare for the next day. She said her bosses knew they could depend on her. No one filled salt shakers or folded napkins like our mama. When she dyed her hair jet black, everyone at work told her she could pass for Elizabeth Taylor. Mama was really proud of that.

When she had a day off, she liked to drink beer and listen to Jim Reeves' records. She told us she wasn't happy and she could have done so much more with her life if she hadn't married young and had so many kids. Not counting miscarriages, she bore six, and only Little Larry had died. When she said all that, we children felt bad and wished we could do something to make her happy. We didn't know what.

Daddy had many things to do besides stay at home. Occasionally, when he went bowling, he took one of us and gave us a dollar. Our daddy had important friends who all played golf together. We thought our father was handsome, except for his gigantic ears, and was possibly the smartest man in the universe because he read many classic books. After he read them, he lined them up in the living room in the book-cases he had built. There they remained, looking large and impressive, next to the fireplace we never used.

Daddy called Diane by her Irish confirmation name, Brigid. She preferred that name and wished she could change her name legally. He called me by my Irish middle name, Eileen. I hated that name. For me, it was just more name confusion. The nuns wouldn't call me Billie because it wasn't a female saint's name, and so I was stuck with Eileen until I graduated from the eighth grade and went to public high school.

For confirmation, I chose Theresa, meaning "the little flower," which made sense to me. A flower is always a flower. It is never a plant one day and something else the next. My confirmation certificate says I am some-body called Eileen Theresa Hughes. After I saw the *Wizard of Oz*, I made up my mind once and for all what I wanted to be called. That's because I discovered a Hollywood movie star with my name. Billie Burke played the part of Glenda, the good witch. Without Glenda, Dorothy might never have returned to Kansas.

Since you never could be sure if a house might fall out of the sky and land on your head in Oz, I had a brilliant idea. If some unfortunate thing happened to Billie Burke, I could be a stand in and save the studio money. They would have to erase only her last name and replace it with mine on the programs. I practiced saying her part.

It was settled. My name was Billie. I didn't care what the nuns or Daddy called me. Anyway, poor Daddy could never figure out if my name was Dear God, Heaven Help Me, or What Have I Done?

My appearance was lacking in comparison to Diane's. She had lovely, thick dark hair like Daddy's. My hair was blonde and wild. I ironed it on the ironing board and plastered it down to hide my jug ears. Diane had eyebrows. What little eyebrows I had were so blonde, it appeared that my forehead came all the way down to my eyes. The gap between my front teeth was so wide, I could stick a straw through it and suck up water without opening my mouth. Furthermore, I had two backs, yet, for some reason the boys did notice me and thought I was cute—not ravishing, but cute. Cute was good.

After Diane left for nurse's training, I had to be the mother and cook. I struggled to fill Diane's shoes. I didn't even care to walk to the grocery store. I much rather wanted to visit Anne's Soda Shop next to the grocer. Listening to the jukebox and watching the teens was definitely more fun than cooking and cleaning. I missed Diane. Among other things, she could always pull together a good meal. When Mama forgot to leave the two dollars, it was a challenge for me to find something to feed my brother and sisters. I really wasn't ready to be the mama yet.

CHAPTER 5

The Bravest Brave

Before I was ten, our kitchen cupboards weren't always bare, and our Mama could be a very good cook. She preserved pickles, tomatoes, beans, and homemade jellies and jam. She also made cakes and real fudge. Sometimes she crocheted sweaters and dainty little scarves for the tables or sewed dresses for Diane, Kathleen, and me. But after Alice was born, nothing filled the emptiness we all felt.

It all started with Mama saying she needed a washing machine. The next thing we knew, she went to work as a waitress at the H&H Drive-In on Little Creek Road. Soon after that, she went to work at Burrough's, and then The Black Angus, where she stayed for a long time. At first she tried hard to be both a good mama and a good waitress, but she stayed at work later and later, until we didn't see her very much except on her day off. After a while, even that stopped because Mama had many new friends. All the little problems Mama and Daddy had before that, became big problems. They drifted further apart.

Our mother's family did their best to help. They made us feel loved, and we loved them in return. By the time we had lost most of my mother's time and attention, my favorite uncle, Johnny, was back in town. I loved his visits. He could sing and yodel better than Eddy Arnold. When Mama announced Uncle Johnny was visiting that first time, I spent hours searching for something special to wear and fastened it all together with a big pin. When he scooped me into his arms, the pin snapped open and poked a hole in my side, but I didn't care. I wished he would hug me forever. Daddy said he loved Uncle Johnny like his own son. He also said that if Johnny had a dime and you needed a nickel, he'd give you his dime.

When Mama's family visited, she was always happy, especially when Granddaddy came. Sometimes on her day off, they sat in the kitchen, drank beer, and ate crabs. After Granddaddy was full of crabs, he would line the kids on the couch and tell a story. First he educated us about the different tribes of Indians who lived where he had grown up in Oregon. Then he told us about one of the several times he had been captured. He hadn't been kidnapped simply because he was an ordinary boy. Rather, the Indians watched him grow and saw how smart and brave he was. The more beer he drank, the braver he got. Then he'd tell us about the blood rituals that made him a brother to the chief's own son. He had learned how to be a good fisherman from the Indians and could spear a fish with an arrowhead attached to a pole which he could make himself if he had to. Granddaddy had wanted to run away with the Flathead Indians, but his mama sent him to an Illinois farm as an indentured servant, where he helped with the crops.

After the stories, Granddaddy gave us each a shiny new dime. One night, Jimmy said Granddaddy was angry with him and wasn't going to let him hear the story or give him a dime, and he, Jimmy, was going to take mine. But I fooled him and swallowed it. I was fine, but I was really sick of Jimmy. I was glad he wasn't the only one around who was my age.

There were lots of really nice kids on Lesner Avenue, and they had great parents who were good to me and my siblings.

Everybody liked Mr. Arrington. He had four children when his wife died. I never met her, but her oldest daughter, Jeannie, showed me her cedar chest. We sat on the floor and looked at Mrs. Arrington's clothes and Bible. The reverent way Jeannie whispered "my mother" was almost like a prayer. Her baby sister, Rebecca, lived with her grandparents. Besides Jeannie, there were two brothers. Jimmy, the firstborn, got his arm caught in a wringer washing machine and had a big scar from his wrist to his elbow. One day, on Uncle Eddie's vacant lot, the younger brother, Tommy, gave me a cigar band ring and vowed to love me forever.

Jeannie was her daddy's pet. Sometimes I wished that I were Jeannie. Her father was so kind when she got poison ivy all over her body. He bought a whole gallon of ice cream just for her. I rubbed poison ivy all over myself and even ate some, but I didn't get one bump.

I loved to hear Jeannie sing as she sat on her porch swing at night. She could be heard all through the neighborhood, "Give me oil in my lamp, keep me burning."

Our neighbors to the right were Mrs. Sommers, her bachelor son, Stanley, and little Ann Lee. Mrs. Sommers's famous apple strudel could be smelled clear down to Old Ocean View Road. My nose led me to her house before anyone else could get there ahead of me.

I'd say something like, "Your house smells great today, Mrs. Sommers."

"I just made a fresh batch of strudel. Care to join me?"

"Don't mind if I do."

In her kitchen she had already set a place for me. While I enjoyed the strudel, she told me how Mr. Sommers had dropped over from a heart attack right next to his car. Then she told how she had nearly joined her departed husband. She had inhaled smoke from her burning pile of leaves that included poison ivy. Mrs. Sommers was someone you could count on. The strudel—and her stories—were always the same.

She never explained why Stanley had never married; she did say she didn't know what she would do without him. Mama said Stanley suffered from a broken heart. I thought, *If my mama made strudel like his mama, I wouldn't ever leave home either.*

Next to the Sommers lived the Boomers. Mrs. Boomer loved to see folks having a great time. She had parties at her house to entertain and feed them. All the guests waited for Cybil Boomer to play the piano and sing. Closing her eyes, she threw back her head, "Nothing could be finer than to be in Carolina in the morning. . . ."[1] She sang her heart out, mostly songs about Carolina, because most of her relatives were Carolinians. The crowd clapped and hollered, "More! More!" And she'd keep on playing, because that's how she was.

Mrs. Boomer had an older daughter, Janet Dixon, and two younger children, Michael and Diana. Michael was the most handsome boy I had ever seen. I never had the right words to say to him, so I didn't say anything. Mr. Boomer was a cabinetmaker. Sometimes I played with

Diana's dollhouse that her daddy had made for her. It was like a real house, except smaller. It had particularly beautiful cabinets. The kitchen could have come out of a magazine.

The Boomers were the only people on our block, or anywhere else I knew of in Norfolk, who had a basement, which wasn't good because you could hear Mr. Boomer fussing for miles every time it rained and the basement flooded. The last time I was allowed to play with Diana, her mama got upset. Diana had found a pack of Lucky Strike cigarettes and she and I went down to that basement, puffed away, and left the evidence.

Diana Boomer had it all, the best of everything. Sometimes I wished that dollhouse were mine. Later, when I learned she had faced some very trying times, I didn't want to trade places with her anymore.

Before we got too big for such things, we neighborhood kids put on shows in the warm weather. Our stage was made from plywood, and the curtain was an old navy blanket. My sister Diane was the star. She could wrap her leg around the top pole of Mabel Coverdale's swing set and do flips, one after another. The kids brought Kool-Aid and cookies, and each one performed his or her special act.

Martha Shriner, my sister Kathleen's friend, tap danced. Mabel Coverdale recited a poem. Kathleen did her own dance routine. Joe could quick draw from his Roy Roger's holster and twirl the gun 'round and 'round his finger. Jeannie sang her "burning" song. Then we went out to the street, where I demonstrated my skill of getting from the front to the back of a moving bicycle. I crawled across one of the Arrington brothers, without holding on, while they took turns pedaling.

After a while, a new family moved to Lesner Avenue. The Ogdens were Catholics, like us, and had four kids—Maureen, Colleen, Earl Wade Kevin, and Kathleen. Mrs. Ogden was a good mama and did her best for her kids. Mr. Ogden was mean to Earl Wade Kevin, whom we all called Butch. He threw rakes and shovels—and anything else he could get his hands on—at Butch. Daddy told me Mr. Ogden had served in the navy's submarine service and had gone wacky from staying under the water for long periods of time.

Butch and I sneaked into Mr.Ogden's shed and kissed each other until our lips were chapped and hurt. We planned on running away and having a house full of Ogdens. We vowed we'd never throw stuff at our kids. We had such fun picking out all the names of our children. That was until Butch discovered cars and started working on engines all day long. After that we didn't go to the shed anymore. My lips healed, and I pretended not to care.

Directly across the street was the family of Roscoe T. Burchfield. I liked to say his name over and over; it sounded like a name someone had put a lot of thought into. Mary Burchfield had the best strawberries in her lovely garden. Her fruit trees were big enough to hide in. I could lay up in a tree at night, reach out, and pick the apples or pears, feasting until I couldn't hold any more. Sometimes I went home and threw up.

Mrs. Burchfield's strawberry patch was outside her window. More than once, I crawled on my stomach and just lay in the patch, stuffing myself with those glorious berries. As hard as I tried, I couldn't look her in the eyes.

Twenty years later, I visited her and apologized for being a thieving fruit snatcher. She said she got the biggest kick from watching me slither around her garden.

"Are you telling me you weren't mad?" I asked.

"Lord, no, honey," she laughed. "I'd never be angry at anyone for taking food."

She knew I was growing up hungry.

In fact, she admitted she looked forward to my antics every season. Then she hugged me and gave me a bag full of flower bulbs.

That wasn't the only time I was a sticky fingersmith. Besides Diane's socks, I picked up a can of money from a church. For ages I worried I'd be scourged with a lamentable dispensation. Even so, I wanted to see my little sister Alice smile. She didn't have a mama since ours went to work. Our mother still slept at home, but she never came home, which was entirely different. So I dressed Alice and took her to Ocean View Amusement Park. When I put her on a kiddy ride and saw her searching the crowd for me and laughing, I cried. We had the time of our lives, stuffing ourselves full of hot dogs, popcorn, and cold drinks. Alice even giggled when we got cotton candy all over our faces.

Later I prayed to God for forgiveness for stealing the can of money, promising when I grew up to pay it back. I sent it to the Salvation Army.

The year I was ten and my sister Kathleen was five, a terrible thing happened in Roscoe T. Burchfield's house. Mr. Burchfield landed an out-of-state job and rented out his house for two years. A navy couple with two little boys moved in.

The trouble started innocently enough. One day the mother asked me to babysit. "You're good with my boys," she said, "and I'll pay you." I couldn't believe how much money she offered just for playing with kids. I was so happy, I cleaned her kitchen to a shine.

Then one day I went to see her, and she was gone. When her husband told me she had taken the children and left him. I said I'd clean the kitchen for free. While I was cleaning, he took a shower. Coming out of the bathroom wearing only a towel, he sat on the couch and asked me to sit beside him.

I did.

He hugged me and told me he missed his family. Then he kissed me like they do in Hollywood and picked me up and took me to his bed and tried to do more, saying he loved me so much. Although he was very heavy, I pushed him and kicked and cried and got out of there.

Soon after, my sister Kathleen started acting strange. Before long, our Daddy knew something was wrong. Kathleen told; I told. Daddy made a phone call. Then a car filled with men from Navy Intelligence came to our house and talked and talked. Kathleen and I were scared.

Since Kathleen was only five, the men said I had to be brave and go to a place and tell some more people what had happened. Once, in a big room at that place, Daddy's shoulders slouched; he hung his head and cried. But he said it was very important that I tell the truth, because a man's life was at stake.

I knew what he was trying to tell me, so I put my hand on the Holy Bible, and I did tell the truth, the whole truth, and nothing but the truth, so help me God. The hardest part was pointing my finger at the man who lived across the street.

Afterward, for the first time ever, my daddy said he was proud of me for telling the truth.

I guess I had been brave, like my granddaddy. Certainly it was God who upheld me.

Even so, I felt terrible for a long time after that.

CHAPTER 6

The Man with No Feet

For the longest time, I couldn't look at the house where that navy man had lived. Kathleen and I had nightmares. She often awoke, screaming. I wondered if she, like I, dreamt of wild animals chasing her. We never talked about the incident. Life was to go back to normal, but it didn't. I feared that man might find and harm us, and I struggled to understand why people did bad things to others, especially children.

Sometimes I wanted to tell somebody, like Mrs. Coverdale, whose husband Charley was a preacher with a smile and a nod for everyone. There was just something about them. Once again, the small unknowing kindnesses of our neighbors brought security into my chaotic world and gave me enough lift to keep on keepin' on.

When I was a teenager, Mrs. Coverdale saw me sitting in a car with a boy, and she called Mama. She was just looking out for me, but I was angry. Even though I liked Mrs. Coverdale, I still couldn't help being mischievous. One night, as she hosted a ladies' Bible study at her house, I called the Bay Drug Store, asking them to deliver a carton of cigarettes and six cans of beer to her house right away. Fortunately, the store did not deliver my order. If Mrs. Coverdale had found out, I might never have enjoyed anymore of her cookies or pie.

All in all, I thought our neighborhood was a good place. The bad people didn't stay long, but the good ones did, like old Mr. Nansteel. He strolled up and down the street, not really going anywhere. The poor man's hands shook when he stopped and patted my head. You never heard him moan or complain. Sweet Mrs. Nansteel dressed like Harriet Nelson. When I visited, she placed goodies and cool drinks on a tray with a pretty scarf underneath the plate and glasses. Their son, Gene, worked at Krispy Kreme Donuts. Everyone said he was a little "touched in the head" because of something that happened to him during the war. Nobody said what it was, and I never asked. It didn't matter. He was kind to me and brought his mother boxes and boxes of donuts.

Another old man lived on our street, way at the end, close to Old Ocean View Road. His house, no bigger than a shed, stood behind the house of his son. The old man was happy just living close to his family. He read books from morning 'till night; they were stacked high, lining the walls of his little home. I never knew whom the old man was going to be when I came calling; he'd pretend to be characters from his books, making the stories come alive and transporting us to strange, exciting places. Sometimes we were lost at sea or visiting kings in fine robes at English castles. We rode chariots drawn by beautiful horses on holy ground. We fought wars for love of God and country, changing history because men in our make believe saw that honor was better than glory.

With each visit, the man picked up the story right where we had left off. He said my visits were a bright spot in his life. When it was time for me to leave, he shook my hand, and in his palm was a lovely roll of Necco Wafers just for me. I wonder if he ever knew those visits were a bright spot in my life too.

The Dollars lived beside the old man's shed. Mr. Dollar made a garage apartment for his mother. Old Mrs. Dollar's little room was filled with pictures in pretty frames, lace curtains, doilies, and mints in dainty dishes that looked as if they would break if you looked at them too hard. Every time I called on her, she brought out her picture books and told me how things were when she was young. I loved those stories, even though I heard them a zillion times. She always forgot that I had seen the books, but I pretended it was the first time, because her eyes lit up. I could imagine her as the beautiful young girl wearing all the nice clothes in the pictures. Several young men had asked for her hand.

Old Mrs. Dollar always cried when I had to leave. After she died, I thought about her when I passed by the little garage apartment. I wouldn't mind seeing her picture books just one more time.

Things were changing, and we were growing up. Some neighborhood kids didn't even have time to play. Clara Ann Wendler, for example, had piano lessons that took up most of her afternoons. She was the only kid with braces that I had ever seen. I wished that I could have braces because of the gap between my front teeth, but I never went to a dentist.

The Wendlers were the only Lutherans on our street. They spent more time in church than we did, which is hard to believe. They also went to restaurants for Sunday dinner. Clara was an only child, but her family did so much together, she didn't have time to think what it might be like with siblings.

We couldn't go to school with the kids on Lesner Avenue, who seemed to have more fun. Daddy insisted we attend Catholic school. At Holy Trinity, a priest sat at the nun's desk in our classroom at the start of each month to collect tuition. I wanted to be anywhere but in that room. As he called each student's name, I tried hard to think of some excuse as to why I never had the money. When it was my turn at the desk, though, I just mumbled and wanted to crawl under the floor. The other kids avoided me until they forgot. I tried to pretend that it didn't matter.

Because we didn't get enough to eat at home, I got dizzy in church and fainted regularly. We went to church every morning during the many religious seasons such as Advent, Lent and Easter. I had keeled over so many times, I knew when it was coming. Then I made a big production of it, hoping for an extra donut. Most days it worked like a charm. I took my good old time dunking those donuts in delicious hot chocolate. It tasted like heaven—and it kept me out of class.

Some of the students at Holy Trinity invited me to spend weekends with them. Janice Lustig came from a lovely family. At dinner, they all sat around the table and talked and laughed. Janice's parents asked their children what they were learning and doing. It was nice to be part of a happy family, even for just a little while.

Once Janice had a boil on her leg. She squirmed and fussed when her mother stuck a needle in it and cleaned it out. Mrs. Lustig was very careful, but I thought Janice was dying the way she carried on. I wouldn't have minded the pain of a boil one bit if Mrs. Lustig had held and patted me like she did Janice.

Asking my daddy for money was like trying to squeeze blood out of a turnip. He always had something clever to say when I whined. His favorite saying was: "I felt sorry for myself because I didn't have any shoes to wear until I met a man who had no feet." I failed to see what that story had to do with sanitary napkins or school supplies. He and I went 'round and 'round like the boxers he loved to watch so much, and I defied him every chance I got.

Every so often, if we had money, Kathleen and I skipped school. It was always my idea. At the bus stop, I'd flip a coin. I'd say, "Heads we go to school, tails we go to the movies." If it didn't come out right the first time, I'd take the best three out of five. We were rarely caught because no one was ever home long enough to find out.

Grandmama saw us at the gas station on Fisherman's Road once and told Mama we were skipping. What she didn't see was the chocolate pie we had just pinched from Frizzel's Market. Old man Frizzel chased me around his chopping block in the back of his store while Kathleen grabbed the goods. I rationalized that it was not a mortal sin because that pie was covered with mold. Besides, we were hungry. We were always hungry.

When Mama did buy a quart of milk and a box of cereal, she expected it to last a week, but we consumed it in one day. She called us "Goops" and said she was sick of spending her hard-earned money on food we ate like hogs. Sometimes we were so hungry we put oleo on bread and sprinkled it with sugar. One of Mama's friends shared her endless supply of sweet potatoes with us. We peeled and ate them raw, since we didn't know how to cook. We learned not to ask Mama to buy us any food. We couldn't stand her wrath and name-calling. When my stomach wouldn't take no for an answer, I just strolled down our street at dinnertime.

During my high-school years, Aunt Edna left Uncle Eddie and ran off with a man she met while on a bowling tournament. She left my two cousins, Myrna and Marilyn with their father. Uncle Eddie eventually married a lady named Ann, a friend of Aunt Edna's who was in the same bowling league.

Ann had been married before but didn't have any children. They were so surprised to discover that she was finally going to have a baby.

Little Valerie Dawn brought them all such happiness and joy. I preferred to be in their home any day. I loved having my cousins living right next door. Myrna had a heart of gold and could sing like an angel. Marilyn's gift was making folks feel at ease and offering comfort. They both were special then and still are to this day.

In my home, Mama and Daddy called me a troublemaker and complained that they had to watch me like a hawk. I didn't mean to cause so much trouble. It seemed as though things happened that were beyond my control. Like the time I nearly burned the house down. While cooking hamburger and soup, I heard my favorite love song on the radio. I liked a boy named Eddy Perry at the time. I ran to the telephone and dialed his number. I disguised my voice and put the phone close to the radio. The song said it all.

Meanwhile, the pan on the stove overheated, sending a wall of fire to the ceiling. Swatting at the flames, I couldn't subdue them. I had to call the fire department. Then I ran and dug a big hole in the backyard and buried that pot deep under the clothesline. When Mama came home, I cried and carried on, pretending to relive a terrifying predicament that had been out of my control. I told her, and the investigators, that I had just happened to pass the kitchen after spending all day cleaning, when a bolt of lightning ripped across the stove. Then I collapsed in a heap and a fireman said, "There, there, honey. You're safe now, and everything is going to be all right."

Mama and Daddy fussed and fumed over the inconvenience but ended up glad when the insurance company paid for a new kitchen. I believed they had bought my story; everyone determined it had been an electrical problem. I thought it funny that the evidence was right under the clothesline and nobody knew. One day, though, my daddy winked at me and said I should go to Hollywood to be an actress.

Rather, I stayed right in Norfolk and switched to a public high-school, where I met a whole new cast of characters, including my first love.

CHAPTER 7

Go Away, Devil

One of my first friends in public high school was Mary Elizabeth Dillingham. She was beautiful. Her thick blonde hair was so lovely that the photographer in downtown Norfolk hung Mary's picture in his studio. Mary was a fun, outgoing friend, who always included me in her activities and never made me feel inferior. She never made one comment about my living conditions or shabby clothing.

Mary introduced me to Iris, and we three often visited the beach to flirt with the sailors. Big ships came to Norfolk from all over the world. My daddy hit the ceiling when I got a postcard from a French sailor I had met during Naval Review Week. John Pierre had sent the card from Toulon, France. I had asked him to kiss me at the bus stop when my friends and I were going home; he had said he wouldn't forget me.

Iris liked to hear about my capers. She could hardly believe that I knew where the devil himself lived.

I had heard Daddy say that the devil was in a bar on Cottage Toll Road. Iris and I spent hours one night dressing up in our mothers' clothes and putting on make-up to make us look older. As soon as we arrived at the bar, our evening was ruined. A man who knew Daddy approached me and barked, "Billie Hughes, you get out of here right now or I'll call your father." We bolted. If the devil was there that night, we never saw him.

Shortly after, Cybil Boomer's brother Tom Hooper moved in across the street from Uncle Eddie. Tom's wife Elizabeth had three sons from her first marriage: Leon, Ronnie, and Larry Tolson and little Ricky Hooper from her second marriage. My fourteen-year-old life changed forever when the Hooper-Tolson family came to town.

Mrs. Hooper could do anything she set her mind to. She cut hair better than any barber and made her own clothes, slipcovers, and draperies. She even made tents and awnings. And the world's best pineapple cake with real chunks of pineapple that slid down the sides. She said that working was all she knew and she really didn't think about it. With her straight white teeth and smiling face, she was the most beautiful woman I had ever seen. Her whole face lit up when she looked at her children.

My brother Joe befriended Ronnie Tolson, who thought his older brother Leon would like to meet me. I knew I was in big trouble the moment I saw the boy who would later become my first love. Leon had the most beautiful blue eyes. I never thought a boy could be pretty until I saw Leon.

We began spending time together right away. I often sneaked out of the house to meet Leon at our favorite place, Anne's Soda Shop on Vero Street. Inside was a pinball machine and a jukebox with bubble lights just like the one on the television program *Happy Days*. After school, we hung around and slowly sipped Cokes if we had money. Doc Silverman, the owner, let me cash in empty soda bottles I found alongside Chesapeake Street. I redeemed them for cash when nobody else was in the store.

It was always the same routine. We girls sat in the booths, giggled, and tried not to look like we were paying attention to the boys. The boys gathered around the pinball machine and pretended not to be watching us.

As far as Daddy was concerned, Leon had two strikes against him. First, he was from North Carolina. According to my father, Carolinians flocked to Virginia and took government jobs away from folks who had first priority. He got hot under the collar if I reminded him that his people came from western Maryland and the hills of West Virginia. Second, Leon was Protestant, a Methodist. Daddy said all Protestants were "holy rollers." His trusted friend had told him that Protestants got all worked up and rolled around, and he believed it—even though he had never set foot in any place of worship but a Catholic Church. That would have been unpardonable. If his friend had said they rolled around, then they rolled around. Daddy believed he was telling me the truth and that it was for my own good. I, on the other hand, made a mental note to find out for myself in the future.

CHAPTER 8

Those Blue Eyes

Besides being terribly handsome, Leon Tolson was smart. He could take things apart, fix what was wrong, and put them back together, especially televisions. He'd stay up half the night in a storage space above his garage and tinker. His mother said he had always been interested in electrical gadgets. Once she bought new lamps with cords that wouldn't reach the outlet. As she shopped for extensions, little Leon came across the problem. With a knife, he cut the cords and tied them together, thinking one lamp reaching the outlet was better than nothing. "It's a wonder he didn't get shocked," she said. Glad he wasn't hurt, she forgot to be angry. Leon loved his mother more than he ever loved anyone else; his eyes glowed when he spoke of her.

When we weren't kissing and holding each other, either he was moaning or I was complaining. Leon was not happy about his parents' divorce and less happy about Tom being married to his mother. I just couldn't please Daddy no matter what I did.

The last whipping I got was a result of Daddy's unreasonableness and my mouth. It had a way of getting me into trouble. My father showed me how to draw a picture of a backwards elephant, but he must have forgotten. When he saw a drawing that I had done of the same elephant, he thought it was obscene and whipped me. When I showed Leon the bruises on my legs he felt very sorry for me and promised he would never hit me.

Then we decided to show them all. We'd run away and get married. Neither of us cared about school. He was flunking because he slept all day and stayed up all night. I was ashamed of my clothes, and I was tired of being hungry and never having money for lunch or anything else. I also knew that Daddy and I would continue in our same cycle of anger. I was fifteen, Leon was eighteen, and we thought we already knew almost everything there was to know.

The first person to hear our plan was my friend Mary. She knew a girl with beautiful penmanship who knew a place in South Carolina where kids could get married with few questions. The girl, pretending to be my widowed mother, wrote a nice letter to "Whom It May Concern," giving me permission to marry.

The second person I told was Grandmama. Surprisingly, she did not try to stop us. Rather, she told me that when my mama married, she had written the number nine on two pieces of paper and stuck one in each of her shoes, so that she wasn't lying (in her opinion) when she swore to be "over eighteen." Then Grandmama made me promise to see her before we left.

Getting the money together was not easy. We hocked everything we had of any value. Leon sold most of his electrical parts; I sold a necklace someone had given me. Gathering our belongings was easy; neither of us had much. My parents were not at home when I packed. I told my sisters that my friend had lost everything in a house fire and I was lending her my things. Lying came easily then.

We kept my promise to Grandmama on our way out of town. She gave us some food and blankets. Grandmama and I held each other closely and said good-bye. There were tears in her eyes.

Leon's father, Edgar Jones Tolson, left his car with Leon when he was out to sea. We decided to use it to make our getaway. The trip to Chesterfield, South Carolina, took almost all night. Tired, we changed our clothes in an old gas station before searching for the justice of the peace. I put my "nines" in my shoes; then I practiced lying in the mirror.

Within an hour, a lady married us and shocked us by saying, "That'll be fifteen dollars, please." Wow! That was almost all we had left to our names. Our wedding supper consisted of two ice cream cones. We spent our wedding night huddled underneath Grandmama's blankets, waiting for the ferry at Alligator River in North Carolina.

How Elizabeth Hooper knew where we were going is a mystery to me. She was parked along the road in Buxton, North Carolina, where Leon was born. Leon was brave; he got out of the car and went to his mother. She reminded him that I was only fifteen and he could be in serious trouble, having taken a minor across a state line. When he announced that we were married, she was not cheered, but neither did she weep, wail, or gnash her teeth. She simply asked what he planned to do next. Then she wanted to know if he had any idea how he was going to take care of a wife, that is, in the case that my father decided not to prosecute and send Leon straight to jail.

After leaving Mrs. Hooper, we drove to Leon's father and stepmother's house in Frisco, North Carolina, right up the road from Buxton.

Minerva greeted us with a smile. "I've been expecting you," she said. When the shock of our marriage had worn off a bit, she prepared a feast and welcomed me into the family. We confessed that we had hocked Leon's dad's spare tire because we had run out of money. She laughed and said, "Consider it a wedding present."

Every one of Leon's relatives accepted me, and we had a wonderful time meeting one another. Most of them descended from people who had been shipwrecked and stranded on the island of Cape Hatteras. They had a unique way of talking, which sounded somewhat British. They all liked to say, "It's howy towyd own the souwnd soyd," or something close to that.

Leon's grandfather on his mother's side had built his home. He even used wood that had washed ashore on the outer banks. His ancestors were French. Their name was Jeannette. It was a nice house with a potbellied stove in the main room. Leon claimed to have gotten his lopsided smile when his daddy dropped him and his face hit that stove.

At that house, heaps of brothers and sisters and relatives were always coming and going. Goldie was the most fun. She and her husband, Bill, made us feel right at home. Goldie's son Bobby was Leon's favorite playmate when they were little boys. Leon enjoyed telling a few stories himself, like the one about their runaway mamas.

Once, as the two boys sat side by side on Bobby's front porch, Bobby started crying his eyes out.

"What's wrong?" Leon asked.

Bobby pointed to the street and cried, "My mama is leaving me here and going off someplace."

Leon laughed. "That ain't no reason to cry," he said.

Bobby pointed again and declared, "Look, there's your mama running to catch up with her!" They both cried so loudly their mamas came back to find out what was wrong. So much for bravery.

Leon and I knew the laughing couldn't last forever. We had to get serious about the basics of living. He called his mother in Norfolk and asked if we could stay with her while he looked for a job. She said we could sleep on the couch. Lucky for us, Elizabeth got Leon a job making tents. Within two weeks, Leon discovered he wasn't a tentmaker. He tried to join the Coast Guard, as did most young men from the Outer Banks who didn't make tents or work in hardware stores. The Coast Guard said his teeth were too bad and suggested he try the navy. The navy accepted him, and in a few days, he was soon on his way to boot camp at Great Lakes, Illinois.

Just days after Leon left, I had a minor problem and had to visit a doctor for just the second time in my life. Unfortunately, the doctor spoke limited English, and I was very naive. In his initial round of questions, he asked the color of my stools. I thought he had flipped his lid. The only time I had heard the word *stool* was in reference to the stools around Mama's breakfast counter. I couldn't think of an answer for the longest time.

Finally I told him, "Black legs with yellow tops."

He excused himself, and I thought I heard him laughing in the hall. I figured he was just plain weird. He returned with a nurse who asked the same question. I repeated my answer. Then they both went out of the room and laughed. Eventually we understood each other.

Leon did so well that he was company commander in no time. Leon loved the navy and had an easy way of making new friends. His telephone calls were filled with details of exciting things that were happening to him. One month while he was away, we talked on the phone so long it took my entire allotment check to pay the bill. My check was $91.30. I missed him and wished that I could go to boot camp. Little did I know that the boot camp of my adult life was about to begin.

Section II.
Child Parent

CHAPTER 9

· · · · · · · · · · · · · · ·

The Tolson Baby

T he next time I talked to Leon, he was excited about the tests he had taken. He had shown a high aptitude for electronics—surprise, surprise. After boot camp, he studied intercommunications at the Great Lakes Naval Training Center. His rate was ICFN, which Daddy later teasingly said meant, "I can't fix nothing." Leon said I could come to Illinois if I wanted to. Coincidentally, I was working at a five-and-dime with a girl who was going to that very same place, and she offered me a ride. The next thing I knew, I was kissing and hugging Leon again. We were in the coldest place I had ever been to in my life. It was so cold, tears could freeze on my face before they slid down my cheeks.

We found a little apartment in Waukegan, Illinois. Our first meal was a can of Campbell's vegetable beef soup cooked in a coffeepot. After the soup, we made coffee, and Leon said I was a good cook. We laughed and hugged some more. Our mothers had given me enough supplies to get by at first. Everything I owned was packed with our household belongings in Daddy's old footlocker.

Leon's classes were to end by Christmas, so we decided to surprise his mother and go home for the holidays. We checked out a car lot Leon had heard about that offered good deals to young service men. A big maroon Mercury on the back of the lot had a sign in its window: Good Deal . . . Cheap!! We bought it for all that we had: one hundred dollars. Then the dealer told us how to get a license plate. We hadn't figured that in our expenses, so we decided we really didn't need one. Two sailors heading our way rode with us and paid for gas. Everything was fine until a state trooper stopped us in Clifton Forge, Virginia.

Our car was impounded, the sailors "hitched" a ride, and we sat in the jailhouse, feeling very sorry for ourselves. What else could we do but call Leon's mother. Leon practiced his speech, got up his nerve, and lost it all as soon as she answered the phone. He blurted, "Merry Christmas, Mother. I'm in jail!" and cried.

Elizabeth and Tom arrived as soon as possible. They never snickered or made comments to make us feel bad. The whole event was treated matter-of-factly, and we ended up having a pretty nice Christmas. Until the night Cybil Boomer had her Christmas party.

Leon didn't want to go. I said I was going without him, and we had our first major argument, which ended with Tom pulling Leon away from me after Leon had tried to choke me. I remembered his promise, and my heart was sad.

Somehow we patched things up and left for New London, Connecticut, where Leon was happy to serve in the Submarine Service. Our first home was a Quonset hut just like the one Aunt Ruthie had lived in. It was nicely furnished with cute little dishes and stacks of linens. In that hut, Leon agreed to marry me in the church. I hadn't been allowed to go home because my father didn't consider us married. He said I was living in sin.

I spent most of my days dreaming about a baby. I had chosen her name, Patricia Ann, and we were going to live happily ever after. Before long, my baby girl was on her way. She was growing in me when her daddy and I exchanged vows, again. God, too, was there that time.

Our next duty station was back in Norfolk on the submarine *USS Argonaut SS-475*. We were so happy to be home and found the nicest apartment on Peachtree Street close to Ocean View. I could walk to the bus stop and go home any time I wanted to visit. Everyone seemed happy about the baby coming. Mama took the time to crochet a sweater set with tiny pink ribbons. I had told her my baby was a girl.

I had no idea how babies were born. When labor started in November 1959, I was so frightened, I kept stopping things up and nothing was progressing. Leon, Mama, Daddy, Elizabeth, and Tom waited for three days at the Portsmouth Naval Hospital. I lay in the bed crying. For some reason, I thought my belly button was supposed to open up and my baby would pop out. A very kind doctor finally figured out something was wrong. He sat on my bed and asked if I knew what was happening. I cried and told him that I didn't and was scared. He rubbed my tummy and told me about the miracle of birth. I was still in pain, but I was no longer afraid. I was seventeen.

Wouldn't you just know, the lady ahead of me in the delivery room was Mrs. Olson and I was Mrs. Tolson. When the corpsman announced in the waiting room, "The Olson baby is here," a bleary-eyed set of grandparents, mama, daddy, Leon's mother, step-dad, and a new father welcomed baby boy Olson, whose parents were black. The group went for a drink at the Enlisted Men's Club to discuss whom the little fellow looked like. Tom was about to say the baby resembled my daddy when the corpsman came in and announced the Tolson baby had arrived. They all celebrated, thinking we had brought twins into the family, while little Pattie Tolson waited patiently for her daddy and grandparents.

Daddy said I could go home and stay with my family while I got my strength back. He sat and stared at Pattie for the longest time. Mama told me that on the seventh day after birth, all my organs would go back into place. I lay in the bed afraid to move, waiting for the mad dash to occur inside of my stomach. Nothing happened, and I thought something was wrong. When I told the doctor what Mama had said, he laughed and instructed me to ask him my questions.

Leon's father came all the way from Baltimore to see his first grandchild, who was born on his birthday. Pattie was wonderful. I wanted to kiss her and hold her close and never let her get away. I sat for hours with her in my arms and sang her song "Oh Patricia, my darling Patricia. . . ." Leon was proud of himself and bored everybody to tears with the Olson baby story.

When Pattie was four months old, Leon's submarine was sent to the Philadelphia Naval Shipyard for refitting. In no time at all, I saved enough money to join him. I was eager to return to my birthplace, because Mama had fond memories of her life there.

Pattie and I arrived on a Greyhound bus with stroller, crib, and footlocker. Our first night in Philadelphia, I made a bed for her in a drawer and pulled it close to the bed. Leon was surprised I could take care of a baby so well. And it was a good thing. In that hotel, I conceived again.

The next day, I found an apartment in South Philadelphia in an Italian section of old row homes. We lived on the third floor; the bathroom was on the second. Through our window, lights flashed from a bar across the street. At the beginning of each month, I made sure Pattie had enough baby food and formula to last until payday. I washed her diapers in the bathtub downstairs and crawled out the window to hang the diapers and our laundry on the roof. When the trains passed, I hurried out to get the laundry. If I didn't, I had to wash them again to remove the soot.

During the day, I read to Pattie and played classical music for her. We were happy. Sometimes we strolled around town. It was a very different kind of place. Merchants pulled their wares on racks right out on the sidewalks. Some sold pretzels served with mustard. There were stores for nothing but pasta of all types, shapes, and sizes.

I could smell the bread stores before I saw them. Mamas shopped every day. I enjoyed hearing them bargaining in Italian. Even though they yelled and swung their arms all around no one seemed to be angry. They looked like they were having a bunch of fun.

Half the time we ran out of money before my check came. Sometimes I had nothing at all to eat, but that was not new for me. When it snowed, I scooped snow off the windowsill and made snow cones with strawberry preserves. They were good but not very filling. Once in a while, I ate Pattie's leftover baby food.

The best treats came in Leon's clothes. He'd snitch potatoes from the submarine galley and hide them in his socks. Or he'd take a steak and stuff it in his pocket. He'd make a game out of it by waltzing through the door smiling really big and saying, "Daddy has a surprise for Mommy." I'd shriek, jump on him, and search for food. After all the tickling and laughing, I'd feast while Leon played with Pattie. He loaded up on the navy's fine submarine food while he was on duty, so he was not hungry at home.

Being pregnant for the second time was no picnic for me. I didn't have many good days. Then serious problems began to develop between Leon and me. He was a loving person who wanted to touch and kiss me all the time. I wanted to throw up or sleep. I pushed him away with one excuse after another.

I was struggling mentally, too. I couldn't forget things my parents had said over the years. Daddy had said I would end up pregnant and out on the street. Mama's words echoed in my head: "Don't let any boy

touch you. Do you hear me? That's all they want. They have no conscience. They're filthy. They'll get you pregnant and leave you to fend
for yourself. You can't come piling back into my house. You'll end up
miserable with a house full of kids just like me." I had a far-from-healthy
base on which to build an intimate marriage.

Then Leon invented the game I called "I'm Going to Leave You Now."
We'd fight about sex; then he'd pack his duffel bag. He'd say he was tired
of living with a cold fish and that he could find someone to give him
anything he wanted, any time. I'd cry the whole time and beg him not to
go. He'd leave, slamming the door. Sometimes he stayed away as long as
thirty minutes before he came back and declared he was giving me another chance. I was always so grateful that I kept the apartment shining
and did whatever he wanted me to do.

During the middle of my pregnancy, the submarine went to the Medi-
terranean Sea on a cruise. Before Leon left, we moved into Merrimack
Park, a navy housing project in Ocean View. We were back in Norfolk in
the same development where my Aunt Nona and Mama and Daddy had
once lived.

Our apartment was very nice; Pattie had her own room. We bought
a lovely three-room grouping of furniture from Grand Furniture Store. I
spent my days reading and playing with my "Pattie Cake." Then I'd fall
into bed at night because I still didn't feel well and couldn't wait to get
off my feet. I gained fifty pounds, all in my stomach. Leon's mother said
I looked like I could use a wheelbarrow. I felt like a beached whale.

CHAPTER 10

My Angel Baby

O ne week before my second child was born, I had a dream that
was more real than any other. An angel appeared and said I was
to name my baby Michael. This was a problem because Leon
had left instructions before he went to sea to name our baby after him if
it was a boy. The dream stayed on my mind, and I wondered what would
have happened if Mary had disregarded Gabriel's directive to name her
baby Jesus.

When our son was born, December 5, 1960, he did not look like an
Edgar Leon to me. More importantly, I was afraid not to heed the angel's
words. So I chose Michael Leon, thinking the middle name would soften
his daddy when he returned. Michael, weighing nine pounds, thirteen
ounces, was a beautiful baby.

When Leon came home, he held our son and said, "My little Edgar."

I was nervous, but I told Leon what I had done.

Leon held the baby away from him and asked, "If this isn't Edgar,
then who is he?"

"Michael Leon," I announced, but I did not tell him about the angel.
"He just didn't look like an Edgar," I explained.

Leon said, "The next boy baby will."

Michael was sick from birth. The doctor said he had a blood-stream infection. I didn't understand how a baby could have an infection right after birth if the mother didn't have one. There was no problem with my blood. Back in those days, though, we didn't question medical authorities. I was sent home from the hospital with a bottle of pink penicillin, which required refrigeration. Michael cried constantly, even though I gave him his medication four times daily just as the doctor had prescribed. Two days after the bottle was emptied, my little baby boy died.

I had heard the garbage trucks outside and had begun to take out the trash, but I decided to check the baby first. He had felt hot through a very bad night. Standing at the side of his bassinet, I noticed the back of his little head looked strangely gray. When I picked him up, he was cold. I knew he was dead. I put him on my bed and ran outside. Someone found me running around outside in my pajamas, screaming, "Help me, please! Somebody, please, help me!"

Even though I had done everything I had been told to do, I blamed myself. Why hadn't I asked questions? Why hadn't the doctor told me to bring back my baby when his medicine was gone? Why, why, why . . . Dear God, why?

The Christmas tree stood in the corner of the living room, and the packages stayed under the tree, except for one. I had purchased a suit for Leon from Sears while he was away. He didn't have any nice clothes, and I wanted to surprise him. He wore it to the funeral.

I don't remember much of what happened the following months. Daddy paid for everything; we had no money. Every time I saw Daddy, he told me how many more payments he had to make. Mama asked me if I had done anything to my baby. Days passed; months came and went. The fog wouldn't lift. I was in the world but not at all present. Every time I took a shower my breast milk shot out on the tile. I sank to the bottom and cried and cried. A great deal of my memory is still missing from that time.

I do remember feeling compelled to visit Diane. She would know what to do; she would kiss me and make it better. I stayed in her house, and my sister was my mother. She seemed so together. She had over forty cans of soup in her cabinet. They were lined up ever so neatly and labeled on the front of the shelf. Peas were lined in rows next to corn and tomatoes. Funny how cans of food represented order and security to me, and maybe to Diane.

Diane had a nice stereo, too. I played the same song all day long, every day for a week:

Better go to sleep now,
Little man, you've had a busy day.[1]

I was lost in some sort of black, dreary netherworld. I could hear myself singing that song. There was no one there but me. Then I saw my little girl. Pattie was standing in a ray of light, her arms reaching out. She said, "Come home, Mommy. I'm still here. Please come home." So I went home. I stopped crying because Leon told me to shut up. He said I was driving him crazy.

Everything about our home reminded me of my grief. We gave away our three-room grouping and bought a mobile home. Life went back to as normal as we could get it, and pretty soon another baby was on the way.

Pattie was getting to be a big girl. I called her Princess Summer Fall Winter Spring. She was my everything, and I nearly smothered the poor child. For months I slept by her bed on a mattress on the floor. I could reach over and put my hand on her to make sure she was still breathing. When I finally slept in my bed, I ran into her room and checked on her all through the night. I was so afraid she would die. I took her to the doctor every time she coughed. She couldn't play outside—she might fall. Other kids couldn't come in and play—she might catch a horrible virus. If she got a scratch, I cried and made her lie down.

Finally, the doctor said, "Stop coming so often. You are worrying this child and making yourself sick."

After a while I did get sick, but not until after our next child was born.

CHAPTER 11

· · · · · · · · · · · · · ·

Little Prizewinner

Edgar Leon Tolson Jr. came into the world on April 7, 1962. He weighed eight pounds and thirteen ounces. Dr. Frank DeLaura, who had delivered Michael, pronounced Michael dead, and signed the death certificate, also assisted in Edgar's birth. When I had recovered from the anesthesia, Dr. DeLaura, with tears in his eyes, carried my baby to my room and laid him in my arms. He said he wanted to be there when I met my son. I was delighted he cared that much.

This baby didn't look like an Edgar either, so I called him Eddy. However, he did look amazingly like Dwight D. Eisenhower but I couldn't call him Ike. Leon would have hit the ceiling.

Eddy gave me my smile back; he was so much fun to watch. I loved to hold Eddy in my arms and sing his song to him: "Eddy, my love, I love you so. How I waited for you, you'll never know. . . ." His eyes seemed as big as saucers, maybe because he was bald. His favorite thing in the world was food, which was his first word. Sitting in his high chair one day, he said, "Foooooood." He sounded like Frankenstein and I laughed so loudly, I scared him.

Pattie loved him and wanted to hold him all the time. She was mommy's little helper and made things easier by running to get diapers and things. Pretty soon they were like two peas in a pod and played together all day.

At six months old, Eddy won a baby contest with the cutest picture of him wearing a little blue suit and a bow tie. What really won it was a tiny hat that looked like an afterthought plopped on his bald head. When the photographer came by with the prizewinning photos, I sat down and cried like a baby. Eddy was a prizewinner and I was so proud of him. It took a while, but I eventually stopped being afraid he would die and got on with the business of living.

We bought our first home in Malibu, a subdivision in Virginia Beach. There was so much to decorate, and we didn't have much money. Elizabeth made beautiful curtains for the living room and covered an old chair with nice gold fabric. The backyard needed a fence so the kids could play outside. We went into debt for that. Then we had to have a refrigerator-freezer combination with a home-delivery food plan. Before we knew it, we could hardly afford to feed Sudsy, our dog.

Somehow we managed, and life seemed happy enough. Leon was doing quite well in the navy. He made a lot of friends who enjoyed coming by the house to drink beer and listen to him sing. Music was a big part of Leon's life. He even played the guitar and sang in the bathroom. He had a song for everything.

My personal favorite was an ode to Mary Jane. I even wrote the second verse.

Chorus:
    She's my heckled, speckled, henpecked, Mary Jane.
Second verse:
    Well, someday soon we'll marry and raise a family.
    We'll have lots of children, and they'll all look like me.
    We'll be so happy, a-strollin' down the lane.
    She's my heckled, speckled, henpecked Mary Jane.

Leon even sang to me when he came home with a snootful. When I fussed at him for coming home in a sorry condition, he'd croon one of his favorite Roger Miller songs. He knew I couldn't stay angry with him for long. There was a song in his head for every occasion, even when I pushed him away: "In the summer time, when all the trees and leaves are green and the red bird sings, I'll be blue, 'cause you don't want my love."[1]

Every time I did want his love, I got pregnant. At twenty years old, I had already borne three children. I didn't want to be a cold fish, but it didn't seem fair to me. Just when I thought I had reached the end of the rope and things couldn't get worse, he'd sing "our" song, with his lop-sided grin.

> They say for every boy and girl,
> There's just one love in this whole world,
> And I know I found mine.[2]

Eventually, though, his big baby blues and love songs stopped getting him out of the doghouse. Pattie and Eddy were still babies. I didn't need another baby, so I stayed out of Leon's way. Pretty soon he stayed out of my way—and out of the house most of the time. He spent more time in bars with new friends than at home.

The wife of one of his shipmates got me interested in selling Fuller brushes. I cleaned houses too. Then a neighbor said she could get me a job at a local nightclub where I could make heaps of money. The manager told me I was attractive and would be an asset to the business. When I left his office, a cute, sequined sailor costume hung on my arm, and I had a job at The Captains Quarters in a very fancy hotel.

Leon was not too thrilled. He didn't like staying at home, caring for the kids. Every time I went to work, he sulked. Then he'd refuse to clean up the mess he and the kids had made. Once, he let the kids roam around while he slept. Pattie turned on the hose and watered the living room, while her able-bodied assistant, Eddy, helped her splash water on the furniture. They had a blast while their father snoozed away. Then Leon said if I didn't quit my job, he was going to leave me. That was the end of that.

My thyroid started acting up. I was sick all of the time. All I did was run back and forth to doctors. I couldn't get off the medical treadmill. My biggest problem was fatigue. It was a chore to get out of bed. I suffered repeated kidney infections and two attacks of kidney stones. The doctors at Portsmouth Naval Hospital admitted me for tests. My Aunt Nona cared for Eddy; Leon's mother and my parents cared for Pattie in shifts.

I was hospitalized for a long time. Technicians took dozens of x rays. My arms were sore and bruised from all the blood tests. I didn't know the reasons for half the numerous tests, because I really didn't care. I lay in the bed feeling sorry for myself.

When I got home, I had more pills to take than I could keep straight. I took pills that my friends gave me too. I swallowed everything hoping something would make me feel better—physically and emotionally. I was depressed. Leon was plain angry. He said he wished that I would die and get it over with.

CHAPTER 12

Every Purpose under Heaven

A ll I wanted to do was sleep. I didn't want to think about my life. Everything seemed hopeless. The children sensed Mommy and Daddy weren't getting along, and they took out their anxieties on each other. When Leon came home, he didn't want to be there. Our fights escalated. He burst my eardrum and said I was stupid and "poor," which in North Carolina meant scrawny and weak. One night he held a butcher knife to my throat and said I was ruining his life.

The doctors at the navy hospital said my thyroid needed radioactive treatments. I took more pills. My periods were irregular, then they stopped altogether. I was pregnant again, at least three months along.

What was happening to my life? How would we care for our children when we adults couldn't care for each other? We didn't even like each other anymore. If I couldn't give my children more than I had, what was I accomplishing? My parochial elementary education had been good, but I was still a high-school dropout. I had no marketable skills.

I felt trapped. When I had called my daddy after running away to marry Leon, Daddy had said, "You made your bed. Now you have to lie in it." The whole time Leon and I were traveling to Carolina to get married, I had hoped Daddy would drive up next to the car and pull us over.

I had wanted him to apologize for being so mean to me and take me home. But he hadn't come, and the consequences of my choices as a fifteen year old were still very real.

Daddy did step in and talk to Leon, man to man, when I told him Leon was hitting me. It didn't do any good, though. Daddy had been guilty of the same thing.

Sometimes when we think nothing could possibly happen to make things worse, we find out we ain't seen nothin' yet. One day as I waxed the dining room floor, a young girl rang our doorbell. She introduced herself as Phyllis, one of Leon's friends, and said she wanted to speak to me. I invited her in.

Then she announced that she and Leon were in love.

"Great," I said. "That's really wonderful. As soon as this baby is born, you can move in here with Leon, and the two of you can raise three kids on all that love."

That lie scared Miss Phyllis half to death. She was sixteen years old; I was twenty-one and felt I had lived a hundred lifetimes. She soon moved to Florida to live with an older sister.

When Leon came home, I told him what had happened. I asked him to explain why he had been seeing a sixteen-year-old girl and what made him think I would never know.

He said he thought I was too stupid to find out and that it had been going on for a long time. All the nights he pretended to be at the Laundromat, he was with Phyllis. He laughed and said I never noticed that he didn't take any laundry with him, nor bring any back. He had me there; I was pretty stupid all right.

Several weeks later, my baby was born. It was September. The leaves were beginning to change, and there was a chill in the air. Labor was fairly short and easy because the baby was small. I hadn't gained much weight; I had hardly felt like eating. I knew something was wrong when the nurse gave me more anesthesia after the baby was born.

I awoke in a private room. I heard babies crying, but no one brought me mine. A nurse came in and gave me a shot, then I slept some more. Someone came in and told me that the baby was a boy and he had multiple congenital anomalies. Daddy came in with red, swollen eyes. Leon tried to be nice but didn't say much. He acted remorseful, sorry for everything. Leon had finally gotten his wish that I would die and get it over with. I did die. Somewhere deep inside me, I shriveled right up and died, even though I was walking and looking alive. Nobody was sorrier than I was. I felt sorry for myself and sorry for my baby boy. Daddy didn't say much either; he held me and we cried together while he sat on my bed. I felt numb. I got another shot.

Later on in the day, a dermatologist came to say my baby had some skin problems he would be working with. Shortly after, I learned that my child had two webbed fingers. I got another shot.

By the end of the day the situation was not good. A plastic surgeon came to say the baby had a cleft lip and a misshapen left nostril.

The next day I learned the baby had a rudimentary eye in orbit. They told me the eye was so small that he looked like he didn't have an eye on the left side of his face. But I still hadn't seen my own baby.

While I was trying to take it all in, someone came with a certificate, saying I had to write down the baby's name for the records. I had to choose a name with significance, something that would make my son feel good about himself through life. Lawrence was Daddy's name, and everyone called him Larry. He had been a featherweight boxing champion in the navy. My child would have to be a fighter to survive. Hughes was my Irish maiden name. I thought the luck of the Irish, if there was such a thing, could prove to be as valuable as fine gold. The humor of the Irish couldn't hurt either, although, at that moment I didn't feel lucky or humorous. So, Larry Hughes Tolson, weighing in at just over six pounds, entered the ring, swinging against the terrible blow life had already dealt him.

The next day, a social worker told me I could place the baby in a home until I sorted things out. She gave me an armful of pamphlets and other reading material. I went home and cried. Larry stayed in the hospital. Leon tried to be brave and to make things better, but he didn't know what to do. Neither did I.

I felt terribly ignorant and insufficient. So, I read everything the social worker had given me, as well as materials friends and neighbors offered. What I learned most clearly was pretty simple: humans, especially babies, need love to survive. Without love, no matter what they look like, babies won't thrive. They don't gain weight; their brains don't develop properly; sometimes they wither away and die.

Thinking about my baby Michael, who had died, made me realize internal problems were often more serious than the external. Michael, a beautiful, ten-pound baby, had appeared to be nearly perfect. Larry had serious external problems—that we knew for certain—but I didn't want to add to his difficulties by denying him the physical closeness of his mother. I couldn't fix either of my baby's health problems, but I could love them, and maybe Larry would live. Maybe Michael's little life hadn't been in vain; maybe he had been born to pave the way for his little brother in a crib on the other side of the Elizabeth River.

Early the next day someone called to say I could get my baby and that a doctor would be present to talk to me. I couldn't believe I was about to bring home a child I had never seen. Where would I get the strength and insight to care for his special needs?

My baby sister, Alice, was the only person who could go with me to the hospital. She was so young, she had to wait in the lobby. My knees shook, and I thought I was going to vomit, but I forced my feet to walk to the pediatric ward where my son was waiting to meet me. A nurse met me at the door; the doctor couldn't make it. She gave me a pile of books, then took me to a tiny room with a little crib. She gave me an appointment for Larry to see one of his doctors in a few weeks. Finally, she said I could dress my baby and leave.

At that moment my brain got stuck on, *Oh, God. Oh, God. Oh, God. . . .*

I went to the crib and peered in over the rail. Larry looked right at me with his one blue eye, and he didn't make a sound. His clothes swallowed him up. I had to get out of there. I covered him with a blanket and carried him out of the hospital.

Alice followed me to the car, and I put the baby in her arms. She pulled back the blanket and never said a single word.

When we got home, I was drained. After I put him in his little crib, I fell asleep on my bed. I was awakened by the soft sound of a baby's cry. Oh, God, what would I do? He wouldn't stop, so I picked him up. He nuzzled his little head under my chin and whimpered. His hair felt like silk; his little arms were the same color as my skin. As he started sucking on my neck, I realized he was just trying to tell me he was hungry. He latched on to the nipple of a bottle with such strength that I was startled.

When he was asleep again, I put him back in his bed and saw that one side of his face was beautiful. His little eyelashes were long and full. I could almost picture the other side being beautiful too.

Then he cried a different kind of a cry. What was I supposed to do? What were his needs? How could I take care of him? What could I give him? What kind of a life was he going to have?

I picked him up and he made funny little noises like contented coos. I held him up close to my face and felt his breath on my cheek.

I sat on my bed, rocking back and forth with Larry in my arms. I cried and I cried—for him, for me, for all of us. He was my son, a tiny part of me. He didn't care if I had a brain or not, or if I was scrawny or ugly. I was his mother, and he wanted me any old way. He needed me . . . and I needed him any way he was. I would take care of him the best I could. If I ran out of ideas, I'd find people or books that had more suggestions.

Finally, I didn't have any more tears to cry. I figured I had better try to help Larry instead of wallowing in self-pity. Crying wasn't going to help my children or me.

In the weeks that followed, Pattie and Eddy must have sensed I needed them to be good. They helped around the house—and they loved their new brother. It didn't make the slightest bit of difference to them how many eyes he had. We had each other. Somehow I'd find ways to get what we would need. Until then, we had what mattered most: hope. Michael had given us that, and nobody would take it or tell me Michael had been born for nothing.

I knew there was a reason for everything. I wasn't religious like my sister Diane, but I had read some of the Bible, especially in my eight years of Catholic school. After Michael had died, I was desperate to make sense out of it. I found comfort in the book of Ecclesiastes: "To every thing there is a season, and a time to every purpose under the heaven: a time to be born, and a time to die; a time to plant, and a time to pluck up that which is planted; a time to kill, and a time to heal; a time to break down, and a time to build up; a time to weep, and a time to laugh; a time to mourn, and a time to dance" (Eccl. 3:1–4).

Maybe Larry, Eddy, Pattie, and I together could find our purpose under heaven.

CHAPTER 13

· · · · · · · · · · · · · · ·

The Good Lord's
Happy Child

Loretta Lynn knew exactly how I felt. Her country music songs expressed every feeling I was living through. The emotions in her voice were real because she had been there herself. Songs like "Don't Come Home a Drinkin' With Lovin' on Your Mind," spoke to me right where the rubber meets the road. When Phyllis dropped her bomb on me about Leon, Loretta was in the back of my mind singing "You Ain't Woman Enough to Take My Man." I thought, *What would Loretta do now?* Loretta had been a baby having babies just like I was. I think she would have knocked old "Doo" for a loop if he had gone to the Laundromat with no clothes to wash. If he had laughed at her the way Leon laughed at me, I think she would have poked him. Loretta was smart. Her music was written from her heart, with her own hand. She could do anything, and she was proud of being "A Coal Miner's Daughter." She had learned and taught the rest of us that a woman didn't have to have a baby every time she turned over in bed. Finally, I got the pill. Stacks of pills, that is, neatly hidden in a safe place.

During the day I conversed with Loretta as if she were sitting in my house sipping iced tea. I knew she was a strong woman. God gave her a great gift that she used to take care of her family and bring joy to this world with her down-home style. What did I have to give to my kids or anyone else for that matter?

My numerous trips with Larry to the Portsmouth Naval Hospital inspired me. I was hobnobbing with very bright people. Visiting with Larry's doctors was like getting an education. I put to use what Grandmama had said I had plenty of—horse sense. The doctors gave me all kinds of books. I read every one at least once, twice if they had a lot to say, more if I still didn't grasp it all. I wrote down every new word I heard during the doctor appointments and checked those words in the dictionary as soon as I got home. I kept my lists of words and referred back to them as needed.

The good news was Larry wouldn't have to spend the rest of his life with one eye. The bad news was, he had to grow before getting a new eye. He was small; the doctors projected it might take four or five years. I learned there were procedures for everything, so I decided to find out what they were and where we had to go to get those procedures Larry needed. Basically, I was simply in search of information.

One day, Larry's primary physician informed me there is a name for Larry's collection of skin birth defects: Block-Sulzberger Syndrome. Then he said something I did not want to hear. The few children who had this syndrome usually didn't live past nursery school because of weak little hearts. Further, I refused to accept the last bit of information—nine out of ten were retarded.

After I told Daddy, he started hounding me to get Larry baptized. I couldn't fathom his belief about baptism and life hereafter. I wondered why God would send innocent babies to a place called Limbo, where they floated around but couldn't quite make it through the pearly gates. Why would a merciful God send His only begotten Son here to die for the whole world and then exclude infants on a technicality? Had the thief on the cross had time to run to church and get dunked? I didn't think so. The thief had called Jesus "Lord," and that's why Jesus said, "Today shalt thou be with me in paradise" (Luke 23:43). To call someone Lord is to acknowledge that person as your ultimate ruler and the supreme one in whom you place your trust. Even I knew that, and from all accounts, I was supposed to be stupid.

I knew Daddy would not let up, so I agreed to a private service, and Daddy was satisfied. Before the ceremony, though, I had a little service of my own with just the three of us, God, Larry, and me. I put my hands on my son's face. Through tear-dimmed eyes, I admitted I wasn't brilliant and that I was afraid I wasn't able to give Larry what he needed to have a chance in life. I said I didn't know exactly why he was born with so many problems but that I believed the pills and medications I had taken, the treatments I had received, and the fights with Leon had contributed.

"Dear God, I am so sorry things turned out this way," I continued. "Larry is helpless, and I am hopeless. How can a nobody like me handle such a big job? All I have to give him is a mother's love.

"Father, it says in the Bible that you will help me if I ask you. So, I'm asking you to help my child, who never did anything to deserve what happened to him. And if it isn't asking too much, will you please show me how to get out of the mess I have made of my life? If I had been good like my sister Diane, none of this would have happened. I had to shoot off my mouth every chance I got and then run off because I was mad at Daddy. Please help us. I'll try real hard to be better. Amen."

With that aside, I got back to helping Larry. Nothing had changed as far as the doctors were concerned. I still would not believe my son was retarded. There was intelligence shining in that little blue eye. Larry had a somewhat wise look about him, and he was responding. He could grasp things, roll over, and scoot around the floor. That Irish sense of humor glimmered too. He was happy, laughing, and drooling like any child. I called him "The Good Lord's Happy Child." Surely the doctors couldn't have all the answers.

For once, Leon agreed with me. He was trying to please me, but something inside of me was still dead to him. He said he'd try to stay with me but that it wouldn't be easy because I was so pitiful. He said I might look a little better if I fixed myself up and that I should read some books about sex.

Truthfully, I did push him away. After all he had done to me, his advances didn't feel like love, and I was not interested. What was wrong with me? I didn't think I had anyone to turn to. Leon's mother tried to help when I asked her advice, but it was difficult for her to instruct the wife of her son. My parents wouldn't dream of talking about my intimacy with my husband. Daddy would have fallen to the floor, flipping his rosary beads. Mama would have given me the advice she had given Diane on her wedding day, "Women are nothing more than garbage cans for a man to throw his trash in."

What could I do to improve myself? According to Leon, I didn't have much to work with. I referred to fashion magazines. First, I bleached my hair—but it frizzed up worse. I bought all kinds of make-up. I thought the blue eye shadow helped the most. I pulled my jeans up and folded them over at the waist and practiced holding my mouth like Marilyn Monroe. Leon liked the improvement, but I didn't care what he liked anymore. I enjoyed the attention from some extremely good-looking men.

After giving everything considerable thought, I decided to find a job and a place where I could stand on my own two feet. I was determined to make it and show Leon and everybody else that I was neither stupid nor a punching bag.

One day I got into the car intent on not coming home until I had a job. Tammy Wynette sang to me as I drove almost every street from Virginia Beach to Norfolk: "Your Good Girl's Gonna Go Bad."

Humming and singing along, I saw a Help Wanted sign with my name on it in the window of a tavern. As Betty Davis said, "What a dump!" It had everything except a dirt floor. Daddy would not have been excited about this little venture, but it was my bed. At the end of that day, I had achieved what I had set out to accomplish.

After my first day on the new job, I was surprised at how much tip money I had in my pocket—immediate cash without having to wait for payday. The customers liked me. I found it hard to believe, but people actually came to that dumpy place on a regular basis. They ran up bar tabs and paid their bills on payday. Even couples came in and sat for hours, drinking beer until they didn't know if they were coming or going. What a way to live.

Making my own money made me feel good; however, I didn't want to work in a place like that forever. My dream was to become a barber. I had gotten the idea from my mother-in-law, who cut the hair of everyone in her family. Daddy had been a barber too in the navy. Maybe I could attend barber college someday and finally make Daddy proud of me, I dreamed. My other dream was to finish high-school. I was ashamed to admit that I was a dropout. Until I could figure a way out of slinging beer, that would have to do, but it didn't cost a dime to hope for other things.

CHAPTER 14

. . . .

Moving On

As I worked at the tavern and dreamed of a new life, I met a man whom I will call Adam. He was the first man to make me feel like I could do more than chew gum and walk at the same time. After I told him my life story, he just shook his head and cried. I learned so much about people and life from him. We laughed and sang, and I no longer needed to cry. When I told him about the beatings, he said no one should have to live that way. His arms gave me strength, and I felt safe there. He said I was like a breath of fresh air. He didn't think I was stupid at all. My heart sang when he declared I had more courage than anyone he had ever met.

Adam claimed that all I needed was a chance in this world, and he promised to help me if I wanted to leave Leon. He also said I didn't belong in the place where I was working, that I could do better than that. Adam was almost old enough to be my father, and he had a family of his own. No matter how many times I tried to convince myself that our relationship was "different," I couldn't lie to the face in the mirror. I knew it was wrong and one day I would have to say goodbye.

It didn't take long to find an apartment. I made all my own calls to put utility services in my name. I advertised in the paper for childcare and found an elderly widow for my children. I decided to leave Leon the lyrics to a song to remember me by: "One of These Days, You're Gonna Miss Me, Honey." Oh, it felt good to sing that song as I packed my things and planned my new life. The next day, a truck was waiting around the corner. I took all of the furniture and my belongings . . . but I left the dog.

Leon hunted me down and tried to talk to me, but it was too late. His blue eyes were red and looked like mine used to look when I cried all night over him. It took him about a month to find someone else.

Adam had been so kind, but we both knew there were things he couldn't do for me—things I had to do for myself. I had to make a place for myself where I could hold my head high. He watched over my little family and me until I could make it on my own. He took my junk car and found reliable transportation. He tried to get Larry help through the Shriners' Crippled Children's Hospital. Larry didn't qualify because he wasn't burned or crippled, but God bless Adam for trying and for caring about us. He said my tattered heart would mend, and I chose to believe him. I was ready to face the world. Finally, we said good-bye.

Finding out about the world is scary business when you are out to sea in a sieve. I found that out at The Golden Triangle in downtown Norfolk. At twenty-two, with three children, I was swayed by the advice of a friend who said I could make heaps of money serving drinks while wearing a scanty costume. In my interview, I was intimidated by the ornateness of the place, but I was hired immediately. I thought I'd drop my teeth when I tried on the costume, but I was desperate to make enough money to support my family, so I took the job in a private bottle club.

Strict liquor laws in Norfolk and Virginia Beach made the club popular because customers could keep their own supply at the bar. They paid for the service of their drinks and the "show."

Toward the end of each evening, the girls danced while the customers whistled and cheered. The girls really weren't glamorous without their make-up and costumes. Most of them were knocking themselves out trying to survive, just like I was. We were all in the same rat race.

One night, a greasy-looking old scoundrel with a "Snidely Whiplash" mustache said he had been watching me and liked what he saw. Sticking out from under his drink were five one-hundred-dollar bills. I had never seen that much money at one time. He said it could be mine if I would go out with him. Christmas was right around the corner. The only coat I owned was a threadbare raincoat with a zip-in lining. I agreed and we arranged to meet after work

In the dressing room, I caught a glimpse of myself in the mirror and cried. How could I ever consider doing such a thing? I found "Snidely" waiting outside and told him I was sorry, but I just couldn't go out with him. What "Mr. Whiplash" said next made me laugh all the way home in my used car, wearing my ragged raincoat. He asked, "Do you know anybody who will?"

I got fired from that job because the owner caught me talking on the phone. I had called home to make sure that my housekeeper, Mary, had given Larry his medication. It had to be given at exactly the same time every day. *Who cares?* I thought. I was tired of being pinched anyway.

The next job was a blessing and the best work experience I ever had. Reisner's Delicatessen, located in a shopping center near my home, was owned and operated by Eddie and Erica Ausch. Mr. Reisner had sold the delicatessen to his daughter, Erica, and her husband when he retired.

Eddie and Erica were the most kind and generous people I had ever met. They knew that I was proud and didn't want charity, so they explained that they had to clean out their meat cases every week and gave me the food.

"It will eventually be thrown out if you don't take it home," they'd say.

My children and I feasted on kosher hot dogs, Kaiser rolls, knockwurst, salads, and delicious New York cheesecake.

They treated me like family. Every week they invited my children and me to dinner. We were never late for a meal at their house. They prepared the best of whatever they had, usually thick steaks and salads. On days the deli was closed, we all went to the beach, where my kids played with their three little girls.

Every day at work was like old home week. Their Uncle Leo, a lovable character with an impish grin and delightfully playful eyes, could make us all laugh without saying a word. He always looked like he was thinking some devilish thought. I loved his visits. Eddie's mom and dad lived close by and enjoyed stopping by for a chat too. Sometimes they would pick up or deliver their grandchildren. They always gave me a smile and good wishes.

When I had to leave Reisner's, I felt like I was leaving old friends. I'll never forget them, but I had to take care of myself. My kidneys were constantly infected, and I needed a long rest to get my strength back.

After I recovered, I had to make more money. From then on, I worked two jobs because expenses were piling up. During the day I was employed at the Fraternal Order of Police Club. The lunch buffet was a snap because all I had to do was take orders for drinks and clean up the tables. My second job was serving beer at night at Charley's Bar in Norfolk. Sometimes I checked hats and coats at the FOP Club or worked private parties in the FOP ballroom on my evenings off. I was trying to save enough money for Christmas.

By then I had moved to a small house with a backyard. The kids could play outside instead of being cooped up in an apartment all day. My neighbors were very nice and stopped to visit whenever I was home. I cried my eyes out at Christmas when they "broke into" my house and filled it with food, toys, and clothing for my children. The refrigerator was loaded with ham, turkey, pies, cake, milk, and drinks for the kids. They thought of everything for our Christmas feast. The cabinets were filled with canned goods, stuffing mix, and staples. Gifts were hidden in every closet. All three children had enough clothing, in the exact sizes, to last for years. Christmas toys were wrapped and placed under the tree. No one had ever been that kind and generous to me, except the Ausch family. They all claimed they didn't know how the things got into my house. But I know that people with hearts of gold saw a need and got together to bring joy to three special little people and one grateful mother. To this day, that memory brings a lump to my throat. I'll never forget the sweetness of that Christmas and the kindness of strangers.

When I hear folks say God is dead, I will never believe it. God was looking out for me then even though I was too blind to see. He provides for the sparrows as well as hardheaded Billies. There was so much more than five hundred dollars' worth of things given to us that Christmas that it made me cry even more thinking of what I might have done with an old man I didn't even know. I would never have to sell my soul to feed my family.

Even so, I wasn't ready to stop struggling. It was a matter of wills. Whose would be done: His or mine? There were still some lessons I needed to learn, some the hard way. Mainly, that His will, not mine, is always perfect.

My working all the time was not good for us. Pattie wandered off one day and was picked up by the police. Thank God she could tell them her name. The police called the first Tolson in the phone book. Leon's Uncle Adrian went to get her and then called me.

Early one morning, Eddy got out of the house in his pajamas. A neighbor, who had my son dangling from his arm, awakened me. He hated to tell me, but Eddy had found a hammer and had broken shingles down the length of his house. I didn't know it at the time, but Eddy had my same middle-child syndrome. He was stuck in the middle and didn't mean to get into so much trouble. He just did.

Something had to change for the better; I worked all the time. I thought surely my solutions would be found in some man who would rescue me. I couldn't see that I could change the course of my own life. The power of the universe was available to me right there, at that very moment. But I was too busy stumbling all over Billie. I had spent my entire life getting things in my own way. I had learned early on in my dysfunctional family that I was mostly on my own. Matching wits and trying to figure ways out of everything were the order of the day, every day.

In a nutshell, my problem was trust. How could I trust someone I couldn't even see to handle my life? Everyone else in my life had always had more important things to do than to care for me. Why would God be different? I didn't question His existence, but I believed that running the universe was a big job. How, then, could my little plight be worthy of consideration compared to universal problems?

Yet my seemingly insignificant life *was* important to God. He was trying to tell me. I just wasn't listening. Everything else was blocking my view of the truth; troubles were wearing me down. I could have saved myself a mountain of grief if I had just turned the whole process over to the One who knows all things. Most of my energy was directed toward finding my way out. If I couldn't find an escape hatch, then some other person would.

At least I knew more than I did when I first left Daddy's home; I knew I didn't have all of the answers. I was slowly realizing that constantly relying on myself only added more flies to the ointment. I started praying, "Please, dear God, help us. Send us someone to love. We need somebody to care for us. We just can't help ourselves. Every time I take two steps forward, I get knocked three steps back. How can I help my children? What is going to become of us? My Larry needs an eye. He needs plastic surgery to correct his facial features. I'm scared. I have some folks thinking I know exactly what I'm doing—but I don't! How can I go on like this? What if I get sick and don't recover? What if I am unable to work? I am so frightened. Please, help me. I'll be the best Billie I can possibly be. I'll start going to church. I'll volunteer. I will even stop smoking and drinking beer. Amen."

My theology was quite mixed up, but it was a start. Eventually He'd get me on the right track. But not without a few more of my own detours.

CHAPTER 15

. . . .

The Big Date

I had only one date with the man who would become my second hus-band in 1966. Frank Smith and I met while working together at the Fraternal Order of Police Club. Frank was moonlighting to make extra money; during the day he was a senior chief in the navy. Frank had three daughters from his first marriage. His former wife couldn't even care for herself due to a drinking problem. One night, while Frank's children were visiting their mother, he received a call at work saying his children were alone and their mother was in jail. He rushed to rescue them, and my heart went out to him.

Shortly after that happened, Frank asked me for a dinner date. On the night of our date, he called and said he couldn't find a babysitter. I suggested he bring his children to my house so my housekeeper, Mary, could watch them all. After we settled the kids in nicely, we went out and had a fabulous time. Frank was attentive and seemed to be very interested in everything I had to say. The evening flew by.

Later, back at my house, I invited him in because his kids were inside. We sat on the couch and watched the lights of the Christmas tree. Then we played a game one of my children had received from Santa. I suggested that he let his children sleep and that he come back in the morning.

Early the next morning I answered my door to see him looking lost in a raincoat that was two sizes too large. I insisted that he and the children stay for breakfast. After the meal, we made plans for another date.

An hour before he was to pick me up for our second date, I called his house to make sure he wasn't having sitter problems again. His housekeeper answered, saying Frank was in the dispensary at the Little Creek Naval Base. He was ill, but she didn't know what was wrong. I changed my clothes and told Mary I was going to find out.

At the dispensary, I told the attending physician that I was Frank's wife, so they let me see him. He was all curled up in the bed and so doped up, he really thought, initially, that I was his former wife. He was shaking and crying as I approached his bed, but he expelled a sigh of relief when I spoke his name. He explained that the last year had been terribly difficult for him and that he was experiencing anxiety reactions from all the stress. We sat and talked, and then I got the shock of the day when the doctor said he was releasing Frank in my care. We could leave at anytime.

An ambulance had taken Frank to Little Creek, so I drove him home in my car. He was still groggy as I helped him into his bed and tucked him in. His housekeeper had to leave, so I took care of the children until their bedtime. The children felt comfortable enough with me and responded well under the circumstances. I prepared something for them to eat, and after we all pitched in to tidy up, I checked on Frank. He was feeling better. I got the children ready for bed, and then I left.

When Frank returned to work, we saw each other, in passing, on the job. One day while I was working in the butler's pantry, Frank came in, got down on his knee, and took my hand. He said I was the kindest person he had ever met and he wanted me to be a part of his life.

"If you move into my house and help me," he bargained, "then I will see to it that your children get everything they need and that Larry gets an eye and the plastic surgery that will allow him to have a normal life." He said there would be no strings attached unless I wanted things to change.

I accepted his offer, and he moved my furniture and belongings into his house. Working two jobs had taken a toll on me. It was good to stay home and take care of my own children. I didn't once miss waiting tables or slinging beer.

Frank was very good to us and helpful around the house. He took no thought about wiping noses or changing Larry's diaper. Larry was his favorite. He even wanted Larry to sleep in the crib he and all of his children had slept in as babies. He bought a giant picture of a farm and taught Larry the names of the animals, a different one each day, until Larry knew them all. He even potty-trained Larry and carried him around on his shoulders.

Frank was good to me, too. He loved to buy things and watch my reaction when I discovered them in various rooms of the house. The day I found my sewing machine, I was thrilled and couldn't wait to learn how to make things. The children all looked so cute in the matching summer shorts sets I made for them out of old curtains. I was proud of myself. We were all so happy, and Frank and I planned to be married.

Frank said he would take care of everything and that I should never worry, but there was plenty of cause for concern when his anxiety attacks came more frequently. There didn't seem to be a pattern to trigger the attacks. After a while, I knew the procedures quite well. I would get a call telling me that my children were here or there and that Frank was in the dispensary. My father came to my rescue more than once, and I was grateful for his support.

Frank's daughters ranged from ages ten to four. My new family consisted of a ten-year-old, a seven-year-old, a five-year-old, two four-year-olds, and Larry, who was two.

Frank's firstborn was Denise, his middle child was Joyce, and his baby was Kathleen. The oldest girl did not like me. I understood that she felt I had taken her place as the woman in charge. Joyce missed her mother, and I was never quite able to take her place. Kathy didn't know what to think and had such a prominent speech problem that I could barely understand her.

One day I finally understood something Kathy said. I was getting dressed when I heard a tap on the door. "Who is it?" I asked.

"It is I, Tatty," she announced. I'll never forget the feelings of love I had for her that day.

Soon I noticed that all my furniture was gone. Frank said the house wasn't large enough for everything and he had simply kept the best of duplicate items and gotten rid of the rest. It made me uneasy.

Then Frank began to lose control of his emotions. He screamed and cursed and paced back and forth, shouting things that didn't relate to anything. After these episodes, he would be very sorry and say he didn't know what was happening. I didn't know either, but I knew it wasn't good. I became worried.

Next, Frank started seeing doctors for his emotional swings. He said all he needed was time to recover from the stress of his previous marriage and not to worry. I was worried all right, more like scared to death. He started taking the drug Librium, which seemed to help him, but nothing helped the fact that I was in deep trouble.

Frank's mother came from Fort Wayne, Indiana, to watch the children when we were married. Ema acted strange but seemed so willing to help us. I was thankful for the chance to get away, thinking it might help Frank. He spent most of our honeymoon in bed with more anxiety attacks, but he wasn't abusive the way I knew he could be. He did go out with me occasionally and waited while I took in some sights. I climbed the Statue of Liberty alone because Frank wasn't feeling well.

When we returned home, Ema was frazzled from chasing six kids, so she left immediately, and my second marriage, at twenty-four years old, began. Frank's attacks persisted. The verbal abuse reached an all-time high. I finally realized that Frank's problems were more serious than I had imagined. After questioning some of Frank's relatives, I learned that Ema was a diagnosed paranoid schizophrenic and had been hospitalized for treatment.

My head spun. I had to figure out what to do. First things first, I decided. Larry needed more than I did at the moment. I would sit tight and see what happened next. Maybe all Frank truly needed was simply time to heal from his traumatic first marriage.

CHAPTER 16

Heavyweight Champion

The first thing Frank and I did was to buy a home of our own with five bedrooms. My child support checks were enough to handle the difference in our mortgage payment, with a little left over at the end of the month to boot. The children liked the new house, especially their own playroom. It was a brand new house and a chance for a fresh start for all of us. Those big dreams faded fast.

Whoever said ignorance is bliss was full of beans and didn't know me. Trying to piece a family together with eight broken parts was stupidity at the highest level. It was a pipe dream. The oldest child, Denise, was always angry, because she saw me as the one who took her place. Joyce was a sweet girl, but she continued to yearn for her "real" mother. Pattie was no longer the firstborn and only daughter. Kathy was plainly bewildered by the crowd of kids that came for breakfast, lunch, and dinner—every day. Eddy bore the brunt of Frank's insane jealousy and stayed in a state of shock. Our very own Tiny Tim (Larry), who needed a stable environment, found himself thrown into the middle of a madhouse.

To keep from going off of my rocker, I had to set my priorities. Anyone would agree that Larry's needs had to come first. He couldn't help himself. My life could be put on hold. I got on the medical treadmill, determined to get help for my son.

I got all fired up but hit a brick wall. The doctors and nurses at Portsmouth Naval Hospital gave me the run around, and it was affecting my boy. His middle and ring fingers, which were webbed on one hand, became crooked and deformed as he grew. Mottled skin was part of his birth defects. The fingers needed to be separated while the bones were still soft. The hospital scheduled his surgery three different times and cancelled each time, claiming Larry had a diaper rash, which he didn't have.

I didn't know what to do. I hated calling my father for help, but I knew I had to. My child needed surgery and no one was listening to me. I swallowed my pride and made the call.

To my surprise, he sounded very concerned, even sympathetic. Daddy said he understood what I was up against. He told me not to worry, that he would get right back to me. There was love and concern in his voice. He called the following day to say we had an appointment at the navy hospital the very next morning. He said he wanted to go with us.

On our way, Daddy explained that he had made a few phone calls to some friends. The first one on the list was a prominent lawyer in our area whose name was Frederick "Bingo" Stant. It just so happened that Mr. Stant was one of my father's sparring partners when he was boxing in the navy. Mr. Stant called one of his golfing buddies—our congressman the Honorable Porter Hardy Jr.—who then called his golfing buddy, none other than Admiral Yohn, whose jurisdiction included the Portsmouth Naval Hospital.

Unlike our previous visits, we didn't have to wait for hours. We were escorted to the office of the chief of pediatrics. Daddy spoke right up and expressed his concern for his grandson. He wanted to know why we had been turned away because of a diaper rash that never existed. The doctor examined Larry himself and said he saw no reason why we couldn't be admitted that next day. Before we left, Daddy, as nicely as possible, assured the doctor that he would be following the care of his grandson very closely.

I was never as proud of my father as I was that day he fought for my son and me. I'll always be grateful to him for what he did. He was a champion fighter, all right, but, Larry "Curley" Hughes wasn't a featherweight at all. In my eyes, he was the heavyweight champion of the world that day.

Without the slightest bit of difficulty, Larry was admitted for surgery. I couldn't help noticing that the cover of his medical file had been changed. It was a different color to distinguish it from the rest. I thought how wonderful it was going to be to have this step behind us. Every mother counts her baby's fingers and toes, but I could never count Larry's without crying.

My dear sweet child must have read my thoughts about counting his little fingers. When I was allowed to enter the recovery room, I saw Larry smiling at me. He had pulled the gauze completely off of his hand. I kissed it despite the blood. There they were—one, two,three, four, five fingers on one hand and one, two, three, four, five precious little fingers on the other. Thanks Dad.

CHAPTER 17

A Gentleman for Mama

Not long after Frank and I moved into our new house, my mother called. She wanted to talk to me privately about something important. When I arrived, she announced that her life with my father was over. I wasn't surprised. Actually, I was amazed they had stayed together for thirty years. My parents had lead separate lives in the same house since before I was ten. My siblings and I grew up hungry with no parental supervision, caring for each other the best way we knew how.

Mama explained that she had once loved my father but that he had killed it with his selfishness. She said she'd go crazy if she had to stay with him, and she wanted a chance to find happiness before it was too late for her. Incredibly, Mama was only forty-four at the time. She was young enough to start over.

She planned to stay with Aunt Ruthie who had moved to Florida. After that, she didn't know what would happen. Mama packed two suitcases and left.

The next time I heard from her, Mama called from Aunt Ruthie's house saying she wanted to come home to Virginia Beach but she needed money. I sent her some. She got her old job back at The Black Angus, where she had worked for eighteen years. I loaded my car with spare dishes, linens, and things for her apartment, her little dollhouse, as she called it.

Then Mama told me she was in love with a man named Jim. He owned and operated a restaurant/bar on the resort strip in Virginia Beach. They had been lovers for many years, but she didn't know where their relationship was heading. Mama hoped that someday he would marry her, but he never did. After being able to come and go freely with my mother, Jim decided they should see other people. Maybe the excitement of "slipping around" was important to him.

Mama was crushed. She really thought old Jim loved her the way she loved him. He had all the right moves and said all the right things. I learned a lot about my mother after Jim went on his merry way. Mama was experiencing adolescence. She was a mischievous child, and I was older than dirt.

During the months that followed, she dated a few men, but no one interested her. Then she met one of the finest men in Virginia Beach. Jonathan "Peck" Hunter was a gentleman. Peck noticed my mother while he was eating dinner at the Black Angus. He thought she was beautiful. Peck didn't think he had a chance with her because an electric shock had left him badly scarred on his neck and chest. The man who had dined with Peck went back to the restaurant and told Mama that his friend was smitten. He asked her if she would consider going out with Peck and said that she couldn't find a better man.

Peck loved Mama and wanted to marry her. She agreed and they were married in 1971. He was a wonderful person and full of energy, even though he was old enough to be her father. My sisters, brother, and I loved him. He was good to the bone and had more friends than you could count. Retired from the Chesapeake and Potomac Telephone Company and a thirty-second-degree Mason, Peck came from an old, well-known, and respected family. He was a widower and father of one daughter, Linda.

Peck was proud of the fact that he had built his own home in a lovely waterfront community. He and Mama loved to go fishing on his boat. He took my mother anywhere she wanted to go. They were busy all of the time with Shriner activities and his Masonic lodge. They went on conventions and had a good life together. She seemed happy for the first time in years. She said Peck was the best thing that ever happened to her.

. . . .

CHAPTER 18

A Fine How-Do-You-Do

Not long after Mama left Daddy, he headed for the hills of West Virginia and took my sister Alice with him. She was only about twelve years old. Once they arrived in the mountains, Daddy had a complete mental breakdown. It took months for him to come to terms with the breakup of his marriage.

The next time I saw Daddy, he had come to Virginia Beach on business concerning his disability retirement pay from the government.

It turned out to be the day I had been waiting for all my life!

When he arrived at my house for a visit, I told him there was something I wanted to show him: Pattie's prizewinning drawing. For months it had hung in Princess Ann High School, along with other award winners. Her picture won a blue ribbon for the best drawing of its kind in the elementary grade levels for the whole city of Virginia Beach. It was a jungle scene with three elephants—the same kind of backward elephant that Daddy had taught me to draw and then whipped me for drawing when he thought that the elephant's trunk looked obscene.

I said, "Now, ain't that a fine how-do-you-do, old Dad? I got a whipping and my daughter wins first prize!"

My father turned to me with tears in his eyes. He said he was so sorry for everything he had done, everything he had said, and every time had he lashed out at me in anger. Then he asked me to forgive him.

"Would I? Yes! I can and I will!"

He stated that it was a wonder I had survived all the things that had happened to me in my life. He said he was proud of what I was doing for Larry and proud of the woman that I was becoming.

Billie girl, did you hear that? I thought in amazement. *Your daddy just said he was proud of* you.

Jesus, I had been waiting so long to hear those words.

We held each other and cried.

"Daddy, now it is time for you to forgive yourself," I said. No doubt he had been trying to make amends even before this day. He had never let me down when it came to my son who carried his name.

It *was* a wonder, as Daddy said, that I had survived all my difficulties. And that wonder was the hand of God, always pulling me toward Him.

Section III.
God's Child

CHAPTER 19

· · · · · · · · · · · · · ·

The Irish Eye

Early in 1968, when Larry was five years old, his primary physician, Dr. Museles, at the Portsmouth Naval Hospital, said my son had grown enough to get his artificial eye. Our whole family was ecstatic; I was singing in my heart.

The day we went to the ocularist, Larry was visibly shaken and unusually quiet. He stood on the front seat between his stepfather and me because he was too nervous to sit.

We rode in silence all the way to downtown Norfolk. When we arrived, the physician tried to put us at ease. Then he put Larry in a huge chair that resembled a barber's chair. It seemed to swallow my tiny boy. The doctor turned the chair away from me, and I could no longer see Larry, not even the top of his head. From my chair I watched the doctor open a box full of eyeballs, all shapes and sizes.

There were hundreds of eyes in pullout trays. I didn't want to look at them, but I couldn't stop myself. Some of the eyes were bloodshot, and some were horribly large with big veins. Some were yellow around the cornea instead of white. There was every color and shade imaginable.

I really wanted to see what the doctor was doing. It seemed to be taking so long. Then, he turned the chair around and I saw my child, looking more whole than he had ever been in his little life.

Larry was rigid and motionless when the ocularist handed him a mirror. God bless his precious heart, a grin swept across his face and he said, "Am I pretty now, Mommy? Do I look like the rest of the kids?"

Dear sweet Lord, my throat closed up with a lump as big as New York City. Finally, I said, "Larry, you are beautiful. You are so beautiful."

So what if his good eye was blue and this one was green. We were Irish. Green is good.

The ocularist told Larry that he would make a special eye just for him that would be the same color as his own. He apologized for not having a blue eye small enough to fit. He explained that until he had the new one ready, Larry could use the green one.

On the way home, Larry sat in silence. I wondered what he was thinking.

When we pulled up in the driveway at home, Kathy was the first one to get to the car. Larry didn't move.

Just as I opened the car door, Kathy stuck her head in and said, "Oh, Larry, you look so good!"

My son put his little face in his hands and cried. He was filled right up to the top of his heart with every kind of emotion one could have in a day—or a lifetime, for that matter. He had been worrying what his sisters and brother would think. He was eager for their approval and acceptance. Little Kathy's sweet words told him what he longed to hear.

The next day we bought Larry a handheld mirror because he was spending so much time in the bathroom admiring himself. It was in the shape of a frog, and it reflected a prince. He took it everywhere he went.

One day, I heard him talking to himself. He was practicing what he was going to say to Frank's mother, who was coming for a visit. He said, "Hi, Grandma Smith. Remember me? I'm Larry. I used to have one eye; now I have two." Then he edited himself. "No, that's not right. Hi, Grandma Smith. How do you think I look with my new eye?" He practiced until Ema arrived, and she was kind. Her response to him was just what he wanted to hear, and he skipped off feeling really good about himself.

The next big event was getting Larry into public school. I nearly had a heart attack when the school officials told me he couldn't go because of his birth defects. The steam started in my stomach; I didn't know whether to blow my stack or go blind. School officials said he should attend a school with other children who weren't "fully developed." "Really," they said, "it is for his own good."

Inside my mind I screamed and yelled and really told them a thing or two. Out loud I said, "My child is not handicapped or retarded, and he will go to this school with his brother and sisters."

Eventually, the officials informed us that we had to get a statement from a medical doctor, saying that Larry did not have a communicable disease. After that, we were required to have Larry tested by a child psychologist to determine if he was capable of learning. Frank was with me 100 percent, just as upset as I was.

When all that was accomplished and I marched to the school to enroll Larry, I felt like a lawyer who had just won a big case. Windsor Woods Elementary School accepted Larry's registration with one restriction: he could not participate in any physical activity. That was fine with me.

Larry grew and did so well in school. He was outgoing and affectionate. Having two eyes gave him such confidence. When we visited Aunt Ruthie, Larry walked right up to her and said, "Aunt Ruthie, what do you think of my new eye?"

My sweet Aunt said, "Larry, honey, I think it's beautiful." And it was—it was beautiful.

He had his one blue eye and his one green eye, and life was good—until Eddy wondered how the false eye was hooked into Larry's head. Eddy was so much like Leon it was scary. Eddy followed Larry, watching him and planning his strategy. How could he get that eyeball out of Larry's head so he could examine it to see how it worked? Evidently that question consumed him night and day. Then, that scheming Eddy told his brother that if he didn't let him remove the eye and check it out, he was going to smash Larry's Herman Munster lunch box to bits with a hammer. That lunch box was Larry's most prized possession. He allowed Eddy to take out his eye, if Eddy promised not to smash the box.

They went outside. Eddy backed Larry up against the side of the house, and he did it. He took out the eye while Larry stood shaking in his shoes. Just then, they heard Frank coming around the corner. Eddy shoved the green eye back in Larry's head and lit out for parts unknown.

Poor little Larry had to go find Mommy. She would soothe him and kiss him and make it all better. She might even give him a cookie. Larry liked to play a game with Mommy. He would snuggle up to her leg and wrap his arms around her and say, "I like cookies" with the cutest lisp you ever heard, and Mommy could never say no. That game is one of my most treasured memories.

Larry found me upstairs washing dishes. He gave me his best hug and said those magic words. He held his little face up and said, "I like cookies." When I looked down to see my darling boy, one eye was looking straight ahead and the other one was off in space somewhere. I couldn't handle the shock. I passed out like a light. Gone, good-bye, nobody home.

When I came around, Larry was crying and scared. He didn't know his eye was upside down. It was quite a while before we got the facts straight. Eddy was grounded for an extended time, for his own good and for the protection of the neighborhood.

Larry had a little girlfriend who lived next door. She was the only kid who ever came over to our house and wanted to play with Larry and nobody else. One day while they were playing in our garage, I overheard them laughing. I walked to the door leading outside to find out what was so funny.

The girl looked at Larry and said, "You know, Larry, you have an ugly mouth."

I wanted to rip off her lips I was so hurt for him. Just as I was about to march to her house and tell her mother to teach her kid some manners, my son said, "You know, you ain't so hot yourself." Then they howled some more. Oh, how I laughed at that! Larry had his own defense mechanism all fired up and ready to go at a moment's notice. He didn't need me to ride shotgun for him. He could take care of himself.

Eddy and Larry really did love each other; they were inseparable. As Larry's big brother, Eddy could do anything. And Larry did whatever Eddy did. I overheard them talking in the bathroom one day about how far they could pee. Eddy said he could pee clear across the room. Larry said he could too. They were so engrossed, they didn't even see me watching from the hallway. I couldn't help but notice that Eddy had a nice steady stream, while Larry grunted and strained and urinated in spurts. After I commended them both for their skill and marksmanship, I made them clean up the mess they made. Then I called Larry's doctor.

Dr. Museles was definitely concerned. He ordered x rays of Larry's kidneys. If it were not for that childish contest, we wouldn't have known that Larry had only one kidney with a pouch like "holding tank" on the side where urine collected. That's why he had to strain to force it out. The doctor told Larry to get out all the urine each time, no matter how long it took. He also suggested that Larry drink plenty of water to prevent the urine from becoming too concentrated. I was glad to know what we were dealing with and how to avoid future problems. God surely guides mothers.

That summer, Frank and I decided that a swimming pool would be just the thing for the kids. Maybe it would help us from having to search the neighborhood to find them. Besides, Larry was cooped up a lot because I was afraid he might get hurt.

The children were ecstatic. After the yard was staked out, a terrible thing happened. Working in the kitchen, I heard Joyce screaming and yelling. I went to the top of the stairs and found Joyce carrying Larry in her arms. He was covered with blood.

She yelled, "Mom! Mom! Larry lost his eye!"

My mind snapped back to the day I had brought my infant Larry home from the hospital. Once again, insanity was a hair's breadth away. I sat on the stairs, and Joyce placed Larry in my lap. The rocking started all over again, and all I could say was, "Oh, God. Oh, God." My body trembled, and I let out a scream from deep in my soul. "Please, God, don't let my baby be blind!" My body shook so violently that I couldn't control my own hands.

Joyce said that he had fallen on one of the stakes. It went into his head somewhere around his eye. I tried to wipe away the blood that was pouring from Larry's face, but my shaking hands made a mess. Larry was covered with blood; I was covered with blood. "Oh, God. Oh, God . . . someone has to call an ambulance! Somebody, please help me!"

Somebody did call. I couldn't have dialed the telephone. I held my baby close and rocked. Back and forth, back and forth. I tried to see if Larry had lost his good eye. I saw a tiny speck of blue. *Oh, God, please let the good, blue eye still be there!*

The ambulance came. We were both going into shock. When we arrived at Virginia Beach General Hospital, they took Larry into the examining room, and I sat in the waiting room praying, "Please, dear God, don't let my baby be blind."

Someone in a white coat wrapped his arms around me the way a man would hold his beloved. He held me and tried to stop the shaking. He whispered in my ear, "My name is Dr. Wright. I am an eye surgeon. I am here to take care of your boy. Everything is going to be all right."

He said he needed to ask me some questions. But before he could ask any questions, my brain kicked into gear and the words came. "Larry was born with only one eye. He has a prosthesis on the left side."

The surgeon needed to know where the prosthetic eye was. I didn't know. He asked if someone could search the accident scene. I called my neighbors. Sonja and Garry Lounsbury, who lived across the street, said they would find the eye if it was anywhere in the yard. They got our neighbors together to form a human chain on their knees, crawling across the yard. Garry found my son's eye, carried it to the hospital, and placed it in my hand. He later said that holding that little eye in the palm of his hand was the most humbling experience of his life, and it had reduced him to tears.

Dr. James Wright did a fantastic job of sewing up Larry's face. When the wound healed, no one would have known that the accident ever happened. Was it coincidence that Dr. Wright, an eye surgeon, happened to be in the emergency room when Larry arrived needing eye surgery? I don't think it works that way. God heard me crying, and He moved the needed players into place.

Larry healed, I healed, and life moved along. My child was doing fine in this world, so it was time for me to think about other things. My dream of going to barber school was at the top of my list. Frank was approaching retirement and wondering what he would do. I came up with a dandy plan. Frank's desire was to get a bachelor's degree in business administration. Mine was to be a barber. I suggested that after I finished school, I would get a job so he could go to college. Frank thought it was a splendid idea, and we agreed to press ahead.

Walking through the door of Granby Barber College was a dream come true for me. Every single moment was a crowning achievement. I was sick of feeling like a failure, a high school dropout, a nobody. The six months of training were difficult because I had so many responsibilities at home and Frank was almost always out to sea with the navy. The course ended with a state board examination in Richmond, Virginia. In addition to completing a written test, I was expected to perform a shave and a haircut on a model. Frank went with me, and the barber examiners were amazed that I had the guts to bring someone with disfiguring pockmarks all over his face. I whipped my razor around his beard like I knew what I was doing.

Before we left, the examiners came to my workspace and asked where I was going to work. They weren't supposed to tell me whether I had passed or failed, and I knew they were telling me a secret ahead of time. I graduated number one in my class. I, Billie Hughes Smith, was a licensed barber apprentice. I would become a master barber upon completion of a two-thousand-hour, two-year training period.

I was on my way to a better life.

CHAPTER 20

Such a Perfect Blendship

Seventeen-year-old Carolyn King arrived at Granby Barber College shortly after I did. The instructors didn't know what to do with either of us. In the late '60s, women barbers were as scarce as hens' teeth. But thanks to the women's movement, the college couldn't make excuses when I applied. And thanks to the NAACP, they dared not brush off Carolyn. Besides that, Carolyn's aunt was on the board of everything in the black community. The closest barber college for blacks was in Newport News—on the other side of the Chesapeake Bay. Mae Bell Britt told her niece, Carolyn, to go right up the street and apply to Granby, where whites studied to be barbers. Carolyn marched confidently through the front door of the college and became the first black person to attend Granby.

Our classroom seats were way in the back, right next to each other. At first, I didn't know what to think. I had never carried on a conversation with a black person in my life. Once, a black family stayed overnight in our house when I was a child, but I didn't get a chance to talk to them, because it was very late. The father, a federal employee, had heard that my father might be able to help him with a job grievance. At that time, Daddy was the senior vice commander of the Federal Employee Veterans Association (FEVA). He acted as a kind of lawyer, pleading cases before a committee.

When the man arrived in Norfolk, he couldn't find anywhere to stay. The hotels and motels wouldn't allow him to register. They sent him to the worst section of town in search of lodging. The man was afraid for himself and his family. He called Daddy, who said to wait in his car with the doors locked. Daddy went to the man and brought his family to our house for the night.

After they left, I asked Daddy why they couldn't get a hotel room.

"They are God's children the same as we are," he explained, "but there is a great injustice in our country. You'll find out all about it when you're grown."

I didn't know if prejudice had affected Carolyn's thinking about white people or not. She never acted upset. Every single day she came in wearing the biggest smile you ever saw. She would get right in my face, greet me, and ask how I was doing. How were the kids? Did we all have a good night? How was little Mr. Larry? She remembered each one of my children's names and ages, as well as other details. No matter what was going on in her life, she would plop down to talk and not allow me to just sit.

She came into my life and gave without taking or expecting anything. All she wanted was to be my friend and share the wonder of herself. Her motives were pure and on a higher level than anything I had ever experienced. Her wisdom was well beyond her years.

One day she invited me to her house for lunch, and before long, her family was as familiar to me as mine was to her. Her mother had passed away many years prior, before leaving behind ten children: six girls and four boys. Carolyn's Aunt Mae Bell traveled to North Carolina and brought the six girls home to raise by herself. Her only child was grown. Aunt Mae Bell cared for her sister's children with the money she made cutting hair. She owned Britt's Barber shop down the street from our school.

A true unsung hero, Mae Bell Britt contributed more to life than anyone I had ever met. She saved six little girls and taught them how to give instead of complain and how to be confident. She taught them that there are good and bad in every race and that there is no shame in having few possessions. Her girls knew they could be whatever they chose to be and that hard work would never hurt them. Carolyn King was the first black girl to graduate from Maury High School, and she talked about her aunt with love written all over her face.

When we weren't studying, Carolyn and I giggled and talked like schoolgirls. There was a spark of life burning bright in Carolyn. Her skin was warm, her eyes reflected real caring, and in many ways, we were very much alike. She laughed at my adventures in cleaning houses to make extra money. One lady threw dirty diapers in her bathtub all week, waiting for me to come and clean. It was disgusting at the time, but a little humor in reflection always made things a bit brighter. I dunked the diapers in the toilet first to loosen things up. I'll never forget that job: gag and dunk, gag and dunk. Carolyn nearly fell off her seat, laughing. The deal was, I could take my kids, we could eat all we wanted, and I would end up with five dollars in my pocket for the cleaning. I could make five dollars more if I took a full basket of ironing home and brought it back the next day. What a deal! The secret to survival was to clean the kitchen first so we could eat, then to get one room clean enough for the kids to play in.

Pretty soon Carolyn understood that some white folks could be poor but proud, the same as some black folks. I learned that we humans are essentially all in the same boat of survival, regardless of color. As our relationship grew, I asked Carolyn why most black folks did not want to be referred to as "colored."

To answer, Carolyn asked, "Colored what? Coats? Dresses? We are different shades of brown and black, just like your people are different shades of pink and olive tones. Some of you are creamy, and some of you are pale white, like ghosts."

I understood exactly. She was not colored like a coat or a dress. Carolyn was chocolate brown, as warm as toast.

Through Carolyn, I learned a lot about how people should live and love one another. In addition to my on-the-job training in a trade, I learned how to care for someone whose skin was different than mine. Inside we were the same.

When I couldn't find anyone to watch my kids on Saturday, Aunt Mae Bell said, "Bring them on over here, honey, and I'll find some way to look after them." She never made excuses as to why she couldn't help. My children enjoyed going to Aunt Mae Bell's house, where they had some nice playmates.

Mae Bell understood that if I missed a Saturday, I would be in trouble with old man Clark, owner and chief instructor of the college. He would act as if we had committed a crime and would communicate with us through his wife, Erma, who was vice president in charge of the cash register. Saturday was the busiest day of the week, and Mr. Clark got a dollar for every haircut that students completed, in addition to our tuition. Carolyn and I were good haircutters, and Clark wanted us working on Saturday.

The children and I loved it when Frank went to sea and Carolyn spent the night with us. She slept in the room across the hall from me, and we talked in the dark until the wee hours of the morning. One night, I asked if she wanted to sleep in my room.

Carolyn laughed and said "Lord no, girl. I'd be afraid I'd wake up with little white spots all over my body!" We laughed so much we couldn't settle down to sleep. I told her I loved her, and she said she loved me, too.

When Carolyn got married, she called and said, "My mother named me Caroline, girl! My mother named me Caroline!" She had received her birth certificate on which her name was written *Caroline*, not Carolyn. It took me a long time to remember to call my friend her real, mother-given name, but it was important to her, and that made it important to me.

Caroline married a handsome soldier named Charles Hasberry. After about a year, little Charlotte Hasberry was born. Charles received orders to a duty station in another state, and Caroline promised to keep in touch, and she did. Several years later, Charles Junior came into the world. When Caroline told me the good news, I knew he would be just as warm and wonderful as his big sister.

Caroline was not a letter writer but just when I needed a loving word, she would call. Somehow when the phone rang, I'd know it was Caroline. When I answered, I'd hear her unmistakable laughter and "Hey, girl," and everything seemed all right again. Someone did care. I had a friend.

CHAPTER 21

· · · · · · · · · · · · · · ·

Lord, Help Me, Jesus

Frank retired after twenty years of naval service, and I went to work at Smitty's Barber shop. I had met the owner while working at the Fraternal Order of Police Club. Smitty, who had frequented the club, liked me and talked with me about my dreams of becoming a barber. He had said that if I ever got my license, to come and see him, so I did. Smitty was ill and didn't work very often. When he died, the job became a trial.

The old barbers saw me as a threat. I had to work twelve hours a day, and they didn't think I'd last a week. Few women cut hair in Norfolk or Virginia Beach in those days. They laughed at me and called me "Mousy." I laughed right back and told them that someday I'd have my own shop.

Things were not going well at home because I was gone too much. My children were acting wounded. There was one fight after another. My stepchildren were difficult to handle. It wasn't their fault. They had been so traumatized by their alcoholic mother that they needed more than what one person could give them.

When Eddy was being himself, his inquisitive nature was thwarted by cruel punishments. Frank said that Eddy was stubborn and that all he understood was a strap or punishment. If a whipping wasn't in order, my son was forced to stand in a corner with his nose on one spot for hours. For every infraction there was more time added to the penalty.

I couldn't change what was hurting my stepdaughters. I couldn't make their mother stop drinking. When the girls hung at the window waiting, she seldom came, and it hurt me, too. On the few occasions that their mother did show up, she ended up drunk or in jail. Often, someone else dropped the girls off at the house, and they cried for days. She even missed their birthdays and Christmas, but I couldn't soothe their pain as much as I wanted to. I couldn't keep her out of jail or make her care for her three little girls. It was ludicrous to think I was even remotely qualified to handle so many damaged children. The scope of their needs was too broad.

The best I could do was to take care of first things first. Crisis management, it's called today. Every day I plodded along, taking one step here, one step there, always walking on eggs, never knowing when Frank would have another one of his spells.

Some days I literally could not think straight. In order to maintain some sense of support for my own children, I had to sneak into their rooms at night to spend any time with them. We had to be careful not to make a noise. Frank became irate if he found me alone with any of my kids when one of his wasn't present. He constantly accused me of playing favorites.

Christmas was never joyous because my children received gifts from their father and grandparents, while my stepchildren seldom heard from their mother at Christmas. More often than not, the gifts that my children received from their father and his family ended up in the trash. It was Frank's punishment for something Pattie, Eddy, and Larry had, or hadn't, done.

We tried counseling but to no avail. There were too many problems. Our marriage had been doomed from the beginning. Some situations are just insurmountable, often because we shouldn't have gotten into the situation to begin with. I wish I had known long ago to pray and seek God's choice for my spouse. I couldn't be the savior of the world for all of us no matter how much I wanted to be. I couldn't even save myself.

Frank exploded over the smallest things. One day, while I wasn't home, Frank almost killed Eddy. I came home to discover a big chunk of hair missing from my child's head. I asked questions, but the kids were too frightened to tell me what had happened. All I could extract from them was that Eddy had been messing with Frank's tools. I didn't get the entire picture until many years later. Eddy told me that after Frank had yanked his hair out, he grabbed him by the throat. Eddy was turning blue and passing out when Joyce jumped on her father's back and stopped him.

My allotment check from Leon wasn't enough for me to get out and make it through a single month. I was not allowed to have any of the money anyway, so I couldn't save anything. Frank required that each month I place the unopened envelope on his dresser. He didn't like my look if I put it in his hand. He claimed that I acted smug, as if I were handing him charity.

Something inside was telling me that if I was ever going to get things straightened out, I had to start with myself. I wasn't happy with me. I had to like the person I saw in the mirror. I believed more strongly each day that there was more to life and that I was capable of more. I had never truly been on my own to learn where my place was in the grand scheme of things. Someone had always told me what to do. First Daddy, then Leon, and now Frank.

I began earnestly praying for help for my children and me. Every night I asked for guidance. "Dear God, I know you want the best for me. Guide me, use me, help me, but please get me out of this intolerable situation. You promised me that you would not send me more than I could handle. I'm there. I am cracking under the strain. Soon I will be standing in a corner twirling my hair and making strange sounds. Show me what I can do to help myself. Surely you do not want your child to end up in a loony bin. You are our only hope. I have nothing to give, just me. I know I'm no grand prize, but I must be worth something. You gave me beautiful children. Please help me take care of them and give them a good life. Please help me show them what love is. Amen."

My haircuts got better and better, and I began to build up a clientele. Maybe I would be able to make it on my own.

Maybe chickens have lips.

I would just have to work harder. I'd keep on keeping on. Something good was bound to happen sooner or later. I was so confused.

At least, that's what I thought until I became ill. My tonsils had to be removed or they would stay infected all of the time. When I was admitted to the hospital, Dr. Boseley asked if I was pregnant. I explained that after Larry was born, the doctors at Portsmouth had said it would be very difficult for me to conceive. I didn't think I was expecting. But Dr. Boseley decided that because of my history, a test to rule out pregnancy was in order. The rabbit died.

Well, what could I say? The best I could hope for was a healthy baby boy. Frank had always wanted a son to carry on his name. Maybe a baby would bring us love. I wasn't about to give up hope. How could I throw in the towel with a new life inside of me? I was not sorry about the baby. But I was between a rock and a very hard place.

The pregnancy was difficult. Frank was upset because he had to go back to work. He treated me as though I had let him down and broken a sacred promise. He accused me of things that I had no knowledge of, and I was frightened.

When he was out of the house, it wasn't too bad. As soon as he walked in the door, though, a dark cloud walked in with him. He was depressed and hated his job selling paint at Sears.

I was too tired to pretend that everything was lovely. He would just have to stew in his own juice. I couldn't help him. To keep busy, I made clothes and crocheted afghans. Mostly I sat and kept to myself and stared at the television.

The kids were out of control. How could we expect anything other than disharmony? They were reflecting what was going on around them. Life in our household was absolute pandemonium.

CHAPTER 22

....

And Baby Makes Nine

Frank Steven Smith III was born on September 12, 1969. He had a head full of dark hair like his father and the sweetest little face you ever saw. As I was being wheeled from the delivery room, Frank met me by the nursery window to behold our son. Frank cried and thanked me for his son, his only son. His tears ran down my arm as he kissed my hand. He was delirious. He begged a new father who was staring in the window at his fourth baby girl not to give up. Frank told the man that it had taken him only forty years to get a boy.

My mother, who had been waiting with Frank, said he had acted like a caged animal, pacing back and forth. She was afraid of Frank and didn't mind telling me so. Since she wasn't offering to pay my bills, her feelings didn't change anything.

We decided to call our baby Steven. The rest of the children were not overjoyed with their new half brother, except for Joyce. She carried him on her hip and was like a second mother. I don't know what I would have done without her help. I loved her for her willingness to take some of the load from my shoulders. She rescued me when I was worn to a frazzle, and she never complained. At the time, I didn't realize how blessed I was.

I had the mistaken idea that maybe the little part of each of us in Steven would bring us all closer together. The rest of the children had so many mixed emotions. I wasn't smart enough to understand the dynamics of it all. What should have been a joyous occasion turned into more problems.

I marveled at how successfully Steven breast-fed, considering the ever-present commotion in our home. The kids' fights reached an all-time high. It's a wonder I could hear myself think. I even resorted to giving them bags of salt and telling them the same lie my mother told me. After they rushed outside to catch birds, I hoped they would stay out all day just like my mother had hoped. When that game wore off, I got out the pennies. I was so overwhelmed that I actually reveled in playing Mama's cunning tricks on my own children.

We installed a door between the two floors to minimize the noise. I had some peace and quiet to enjoy my baby. I loved to rock babies and sing. My song for Steven was "You're Just Too Good to be True." Steven stayed next to my bed, and I enjoyed every precious moment with him. I had never seen Frank happier. He had his son, and I had a baby to hold. When Steven was four months and I was twenty-seven years old, I had to have a hysterectomy. It took me a long time to recover. I lay around for months and just could not get my act together. Frank became more abusive to Eddy, calling him "Ed-*Gaar*" and telling my child he would end up a loser like his father. I crept into Eddy's room at night and whispered into his ear, "You are good, and you are loved."
Larry was tossed aside like an old worn-out shoe. I whispered into his ear, "You are special, and someday the world will see your shining star." I never thought Frank would be abusive to Larry, and when he was, it sent daggers into my heart. My boys didn't have a chance at getting Frank's affection with Steven taking the spotlight.

As Steven got older, Frank took him to a convenience store every Saturday and let him fill a paper bag with candy to show off at home. Frank refused my pleas to stop or to take Steven somewhere else to enjoy the goodies, not in front of the other children. He insisted that he had the right to do as he pleased. After all, Steven was his son, his only son.

Well, Steven was my son too, and what Frank did was wrong. Steven wasn't to blame; he was just a small boy. His father's spoiling and partiality hurt Steven's development. My sweet boy became sullen and difficult to understand. He threw temper tantrums and continuously banged his head on the floor. The other kids didn't know what to think. I thought, *Dear*

Lord, what else can happen here? When Steven was old enough, we enrolled him in a private Christian school, and for a while he was happy.

After a terrible kid fight when one of my stepdaughters threatened to do bodily harm to my Pattie, I decided that enough was enough for Pattie. She did not fare well in the family situation where her stepsisters outdid her in their father's eyes. Frank acknowledged nothing she did as good or even adequate. The marriage was brutal, and my children bore the brunt of cruel words and deeds. They couldn't win.

Pattie couldn't survive the harshness. I called Leon and he was thrilled. He said he would take care of our daughter, and he said his new wife, Karen, would be delighted. Karen was not delighted.

Every time Pattie crawled into her father's lap, Karen saw me sitting there. She admitted that to me later. One day while we sat and sipped coffee, Karen said she was sorry for the way she felt, but she couldn't help it. Before she left, she told me her life was a mess. She wished she had the strength to leave, but in her words, she was "just too old and too tired."

We corresponded, and I sent her inspirational books. I wrote to Pattie and called as often as I could. I had no idea how bad things were in her father's home . . . until I called one Easter morning, only to find that the line had been disconnected. I called Leon's mother, who told me that Leon had moved to Florida. She gave me his new number.

When I reached Leon, I couldn't believe what he told me. It was too much. I was stunned. He could not handle the problems in his home. He had placed our child in a home for incorrigible and disturbed girls somewhere in Connecticut. I asked him for the number immediately.

Old Frank snickered and slithered around for days with a devilish "Grinchy" grin. Every Christian thought I had was gone. I wished that I could make him disappear from my life forever. But I couldn't. Finally he conceded to take me to find my daughter.

When I think about Pattie's abandoned look when I saw her, I could cry. Sometimes I do. The director of His Mansion, Stan Farmer, was honest and helpful. I sensed that he would give me his best advice. He cared about the girls in his charge. He asked me not to be angry with Leon. He said that Leon hadn't known what to do and that Karen was coming unglued. Stan and I agreed that Leon was not a bad person; he was weak and couldn't stand up to Karen because he was a child himself.

Stan advised me to let Pattie stay there and finish the school year. Her life had been disrupted enough. She did have some friends at the school.

I returned for Pattie when the school year was over. The girl who stepped back into my world was not the same one I had always known. Her spirit was crushed.

She was like a little crippled bird without a song. The eyes that once sparkled with life were dull and listless. Her head hung down; her shoulders drooped. I wondered what terrible things had happened. How could I get inside of her soul and soothe her spirit? There was no sign of the defiant child with arms folded in determination. I saw nothing but pain.

Finally, Pattie told me of the horror in her father's home. Karen had insisted that he get his daughter out of the house. The worst part was his telling her a lie that they were just dropping her off at "the home" and would come back to get her.

Leon came to see Pattie one last time before he left. The memory will live on in her heart forever. She asked him if he was there to pick her up. He hung his head and couldn't speak the words she didn't want to hear. The last thing she said to her father was, "Whatever you have to say, I'm not interested. As far as I'm concerned, I never want to see you again."

One day while I was shopping, I decided to visit an old barber friend of mine, Wally Barbee. He said he was going into the trucking business and wanted to sell his shop, which was just down the street from our house. He offered me a good deal if I wanted to become the new owner. Frank was interested. Wally said I could finish my apprenticeship there and do the legal paperwork later. Approximately five years from the time I walked into Granby Barber College, I, Billie Hughes Smith, was a certified master barber. We mortgaged our house, went into business, and I was an entrepreneur.

When my grandfather died, Aunt Edna gave me a name for my shop. My aunt, like everyone else, was grieving at the loss of her father. So much that she was intoxicated. She told me how well she had been treated at the "hairport" after her plane had landed. Hairport! What a great name for a barber shop! Thanks, Aunt Edna, and thanks, Granddaddy.

I had gotten a name for the business of my dreams, but I was keenly aware of having lost my dear grandfather. He gave me so many happy memories through the years that I hung onto for comfort. Now I know I will see him again when I get to heaven. He'll be the one wearing the Indian headdress.

CHAPTER 23

The Quivering Ort

The first angel I ever struck up a conversation with was sitting in a rocking chair in the pediatric ward of Virginia Beach General Hospital. Eighteen-month-old Steven had pneumonia and was not responding to treatment. There she was, smiling, rocking, and acting like she didn't have a care in the world. Something about her was different from any other person I had ever met. I knew it right away. I introduced myself and drew her out as to why she was at the hospital. She told me that the only two children she had were in little hospital cribs, dying. I was shocked. I had to know why she was rocking and smiling despite her terrible situation. That angel smiled more widely and said, "Honey, God is in control here, and whatever strength I need, He will freely give, because He loves me, He loves my children, and He loves you too."

I thought, *How could God love me? You don't know that I stole as a child and lied. You don't know that I spitefully bit off the finger of my sister's doll. What of my failed marriages and the general mess I have made of my life?* My own record of wrongs scrolled through my mind like a condemning list. Then a list of tragedies that God had allowed screamed for attention in my thoughts.

Here I am hurting worse than I have ever hurt before, and what happens? I meet a fruitcake. My Michael had died. My childhood sweetheart had cheated on me with some young girl. Larry was going to need more help than I could ever get for him. My husband had only one oar in the water. Now my baby was in serious trouble and I was not handling any of it well. I didn't have one shred of charm or grace whatsoever.

I sat like a quivering ort and cried and whined and sobbed. Nobody in the world was as pitiful as I was at that moment. I believed there was no hope for me, and I had never felt more alone.

In the midst of her own difficulties, that woman put her arms around me and prayed for my Steven and me. She called down a band of angels to watch over me and to give me the strength I would need to accept whatever was going to happen. She must have known it would take more than one angel to help the shaken person in her arms.

Before I left, she handed me a pamphlet entitled "How to be Saved and Know it." Dear God! There I was bleeding from the heart, and I meet a religious kook. I thought that was just my luck. Nevertheless, I thanked her kindly and stuck the thing in my purse.

I went to Steven's bed, reached in, hugged him, and said, "Mommy loves you more than all of the leaves on the trees in summer," which is what I always told him. Frank arrived for his shift, and I left not knowing if my child would live or die.

As soon as I fell into bed, the whole world caved in on me, and I really lost it. If God really did love me, why was this happening? Then I thought about the lady and her pamphlet.

I dug it out and decided I had nothing to lose by reading it. The words pierced me like fire. I was lost. I did need somebody to save me. Up to that point, I had relied on myself, scrape after scrape. Relying on myself had never helped much with my life's problems. Living in a comfortable neighborhood wasn't the answer. Knowing the "right" people mattered little in the big picture. Education just made some folks think they were smarter than others. So what was the answer?

According to what I had just read, God could love even me, despite the stealing, the doll, everything. He loved me so much that He made the greatest sacrifice of all. My trials could never compare to that. The thing I liked the best was the part about how I didn't have to understand His love. My part was to believe and trust in Him, which sounded possible.

Still, I couldn't help feeling that God wasn't going to get any bargain. I had nothing to give except a trail of tears and mistakes. I had nothing to lose and everything to gain by accepting His mercy and His love. Right there in my bedroom, I got down on my knees and cried out to the God whose love surpasses all understanding. I gave Him my life in exchange for His grace. I didn't feel any bolt of lightening when I asked Him to come into my heart and make something good out of the ashes lying there. But somehow I wasn't afraid anymore. I knew that with His help, I could handle whatever was to be my lot. For the first time, I didn't try to bargain or match wits. There wasn't one single appeal like, "If you'll get me out of this last terrible mess, I'll do this, that, or whatever."

When I returned to the hospital, Steven was sitting up in his oxygen tent, smiling. He said he was hungry for the first time in five days. I watched him eat a peanut butter and jelly sandwich and heard him ask for more. I started shaking inside because I had no doubt that someone else had taken over. All the power in the universe had been made available to me. All I had to do was believe and not stick my big nose into God's plan. In just a few days, Steven came home.

In the days that followed, I began to study the Bible for the first time in my life. There had always been a Bible around, like the big, fancy leather kind displayed on our coffee table, but rarely read. Occasionally, I had read a few pages, searching for a quick band-aid cure for my most recent struggle.

Now, though, the stories came alive with romance, adventure, mystery, and truth, like the story of King David. Chapter eleven of the second book of Samuel was the most thrilling chapter of all. "And it came to pass, after the year was expired, at the time when kings go forth to battle . . ." I still love the way that chapter starts. David was restless one night and was walking on his roof. Why he was strolling there was a mystery. Maybe the view was good from there. Then he saw a woman taking a bath. I think David's eyes nearly popped out because she was beautiful. Her name was Bathsheba, which sounds sexy, if you ask me. Being a king made it easy for David to find out anything he wanted to know, so he sent someone to find out who she was. The messenger returned to say she was the daughter of Eliam and the wife of Uriah. David sent for her. In his heart he was already up to no good, and anyone can guess that he was in a whole heap of trouble. Well, he got what he wanted, and you'd think that would make everything hunky-dory, but it didn't.

Bathsheba conceived, which caused a sticky situation, one that David hadn't counted on. He probably hadn't even thought about what could happen while he was burning up with passion. Now Uriah the Hittite was evidently no dummy; he could count to nine. He was out of town, and if he didn't come home soon, everybody in the kingdom would know that Bathsheba's baby just couldn't be his. David called for Uriah, even had a nice chat with him. He tried to get him to go home. But Uriah didn't do what David wanted him to do. Then that sneaky David did a dastardly deed and sent Uriah to the front lines of battle, which in short meant good-bye Uriah.

With Uriah out of the picture, you might think the story would have a happy ending. But the Lord sent His man Nathan to tell David what you might call a little bedtime story. After the story was told, David saw himself and the evil thing he had done. He acknowledged his sin and confessed in true sorrow.

Nathan had told him, "The Lord also hath put away thy sin; thou shall not die" (2 Sam. 12:13). The "shall not die" part was included because David had said the man in the story should have to die. That was before David knew that the man was himself. Anyway, one lesson I saw in the tale was: Even though kings don't steal strawberries and feel guilty for twenty years, there are still consequences to pay for evil deeds. David lost the child that Bathsheba had conceived on their night of passion.

Nathan had declared that the baby would die, but David prayed, fasted, cried, and "lay all night upon the earth" (2 Sam. 13:16). While he still had hope, he did what he could, and when the child died, he stopped crying. David got up, washed himself, went to church, and prayed. After that, he went home and ate.

When his servants couldn't understand what was happening, David said a wondrous thing. He said, "While the child was yet alive, I fasted and wept: for I said, 'Who can tell whether God will be gracious to me, that the child may live?' But now he is dead, wherefore should I fast? Can I bring him back again? I shall go to him, but he shall not return to me" (2 Sam. 13:22–23).

A terrible sadness was lifted from me when I read about the life of David. He was human just as I am human. If God could forgive him, he could forgive me because I never sent anybody to the front lines to die.

David did me a big favor when he said that he would go to his little baby boy someday. What that said to me is this: I will go to my baby, because like David's baby, he can't come back to me. When I get to heaven, Michael will be waiting there for me. I'll hold him in my arms. I'll tell him how much I missed him and that I never once forgot his birthday. We'll laugh and sing. There won't be any tears in heaven. There won't be any more separation from those we love so much. We won't even remember the things that broke our hearts.

God molded and shaped David with the pain that was in his heart after he lost his little baby. David's troubles didn't end there. His whole life was one crisis after another, like mine. Why should my journey on earth be any different? If God could do something beautiful with David, there had to be hope for me.

It was David who wrote more of the psalms than anyone else, and he wrote them after he had sinned and asked God's forgiveness. He is remembered to this day for the good things that he did and the glorious words that he left us in the awe-inspiring Book of Psalms. David was the sweet psalmist of Israel, whose failures, triumphs, and psalms to God have brought (and still bring) comfort to my soul.

CHAPTER 24

· · · · · · · · · · · · · · ·

Adrift on the Water

Every day I looked to the sky and prayed that Jesus would come. Someone had to come and stop the madness. There was a cloud of darkness hanging over our lives. God had healed my son of pneumonia; would he heal my husband? I prayed and prayed, even though nothing changed.

I searched Scripture for answers and found that Jesus had come to give us abundant life. I failed to see the abundance. Frank told me that I didn't deserve to breathe the air in the same room with him. Was this overflowing fullness? I didn't think so. Who died and appointed Frank the giver of worthiness anyway?

I thought that if I understood the workings of the human mind, I might be able to protect myself from being hurt by Frank's vicious comments. Understanding might be the key. It seemed worth a try. Frank was depressed all the time. When he wasn't in the pit, he was screaming and yelling at us. We just couldn't please him. Steven was his only joy.

The first thing I had to do was to get a high school diploma. I bought some GED books and studied until I felt confident enough. My brother Joe's wife also wanted to take the test, so we went together. We both passed with flying colors. At long last, I had a piece of paper that said I had a high-school diploma.

I enrolled in a community college near Virginia Beach. My customers in the barber shop were supportive and encouraging. We discussed whatever I was studying at the time. They were happy to help with quizzes and homework assignments. Some of them even gave me books to help with difficult projects.

My courses were basic in the beginning. I was surprised that I could absorb all the information that was being funneled into my brain. Then it dawned on me: I not only was capable of learning but also was above average in intelligence. My grade-point level never went below 3.7.

While I was immersed in my studies, I also discovered that I could hide from the world by locking myself up in my room and losing myself in thought. When I wasn't working, I stayed in my bedroom. It was safe behind that door. I couldn't help Frank; I didn't understand him. Several years passed before I came out of hiding. I stopped praying for a miracle that I realized would never happen. If there was an abundant life, I didn't think it would fall out of the sky and land in my backyard. I would have to find it myself. I was tired of my children suffering and me living in fear.

I met a man whom I will call Abel. We went to a quaint little French restaurant and ate crêpe suzette. He was witty, charming, and delightful. I felt as though I had known him all of my life, really known him, at the deepest level.

We carried on a relationship over the telephone for almost a year. When we had an opportunity to go somewhere, I felt giddy and deliriously happy at the same time. There was a new bounce in my step, but I also felt confused. My neck broke out in splotches. I thought I was going to faint. Could I be going through the change of life at thirty-five? I couldn't concentrate on my studies. In the middle of the night, I woke up calling his name.

Was this some kind of a cosmic joke? Why now? Why me? He was the male counterpart of myself, right down to his wild curly hair. I shared my soul with him. He had gotten inside of the heart of me, a place I didn't even know existed. But he and I could never be. Every time I hear the song, "You Light Up My Life," I think of him and wonder why things happen the way they do.

I couldn't get my life to make any sense. What was I doing wrong? Why did I have to love someone who wasn't free to love me? Part of the problem was that I walked into things without thinking what the results would be. I was trying to be a good person, but I kept messing myself up. I didn't know where I was going on the roads I had chosen. Rather, I floated around in the universe. I had numerous spiritual wonderings and faulty thoughts over the years that weren't cleared up until I fully let the Holy Spirit instruct me through study of the Word.

Somewhere, glowing from my inner self, was a sign that said, "Here I am world. Anyone else like to make another gaping hole in my heart today? If not today, then how about tomorrow?" Maybe I secretly enjoyed having my insides ripped out and stomped to bits. Maybe it was some form of self-destruction. If I was as smart as I thought I was, why was I acting so dumb?

I was weary of drifting in the wilderness, hoping to bump into the abundant life. *Dear God*, I cried, *please tell me that it won't take me forty years, like it took Moses, to get out of this desert.* I wasn't claiming to be any leader of the chosen people. All I wanted was to get to the Promised Land.

If it hadn't been for my sisters and their problems, I might have thrown in the towel and slipped right off the track. Kathleen had left her husband, Rick, and was staying with Diane. After I told her by phone about a new shop I was opening on Holland Road with a partner and offered her a job, she came to Virginia Beach. She moved into a town house that Frank and I bought to use as rental property.

When Kathleen saw the shop, she didn't like it. She asked if she could find another location where we could set up a shop together. I halfheartedly agreed, and we proceeded, only to have it fall through when Kathleen went back home to her husband. Rick was a good man, and they had two children. I had really hoped that they could patch things up, and they did. However, I was left with a five-year lease on a shop I didn't need.

Then Alice arrived. I didn't blame her for wanting to leave her husband. He had said some awful things to her that revealed disgust for his wife.

Alice wanted to work with me, and it all turned out well. Helping her kept the focus off my own problems a bit. As a master barber, I could let one student work beside me in my shop. Alice could gain the practical experience on the job and attend classes at the high school vocational training center under an apprenticeship program sponsored by the state. Alice practiced cutting her kids' hair until she was advanced enough to work on paying customers. She was a fast learner. Before long, she had her own equipment and started picking up customers who came and waited just for her. I talked Frank into selling her one of our cars so she would have reliable transportation. Alice was on her way to a new life, and I hoped all her dreams would come true. No one deserved happiness more than my baby sister.

The Hairport, a little neighborhood barber shop, didn't bring in enough money. Since we were bound to the lease for the shop that Kathleen was going to operate, we opened it as a barber shop and beauty shop with the help of another hair stylist. When it was ready, Alice, I, and several of our customers moved to the new shop on Great Neck Road. Frank and I were operating three shops trading as Hairport. In less than a year, we would open one more on Princess Ann Road.

During this period, I received the heartbreaking news that Leon had been killed in a car accident. He and his wife, Karen, had been killed instantly. Their three-year-old son received massive head injuries. Eric would recover, but suffered permanent brain damage. Karen's daughter, Melissa, was the only one to survive with a chance for a normal life. Sadly, it took a long time for her to recover.

We got the news one week before Pattie's wedding. We were devastated. Even so, Pattie wanted to go ahead with the ceremony. My sons sat and stared at the wall. We didn't know what to say or do. Leon's mother was crushed. I had never seen her so wounded. I knew how much Leon and his mother loved each other. I wanted to hug her and tell her that I was so sorry for her loss but no one could reach her. I was surprised at my own grief too. I realized that I would always remember him with love in my heart. We were bound together forever in our children.

Several weeks after the funeral, Leon's mother called me. I was profoundly moved to think she would reach out to me. She said that every time she lay down to rest, she saw Leon's face.

"Is he smiling?" I asked.

"Yes," she replied.

"Then maybe he is trying to say, 'I'm all right, Mother, please don't cry anymore. I'm in a much better place.'" I believed that Leon's love for her was strong enough to reach across the gulf that separates us from loved ones who have gone on to the other side.

Pattie's wedding was beautiful even though I felt her marriage was destined for failure. The last photo in her wedding album shows Pattie placing her bridal bouquet among the other flowers on Leon's grave. Pattie is gifted in drama. She was in the National Thespian Society. I can't imagine where that talent came from.

Because Leon had been killed four days before his navy retirement date, my children qualified for Social Security benefits and government compensation. The benefits would continue until age twenty-three if they stayed in school and could maintain passing grades. If they chose to drop out, the benefits stopped at age eighteen. Pattie lost her Social Security benefits the day she married Tony Elliott.

It didn't dawn on me at that time, but Leon's death opened the door for me to walk out. Leon's children, our children, would not have to depend on Frank for a college education. Their own father had given them that opportunity.

Often faltering, sometimes crawling, I picked up the pieces of my broken heart. Slowly, a new way of thinking emerged. A new sense of purpose and strength inside of me grew. And the drifting subsided.

CHAPTER 25

. . . .

It Came to Pass

The late Dr. J. Vernon McGee was a wise man. He could tell a story and make a point without using fancy words that only a chosen few can understand. Many years ago, he told the story of a men's Bible study group that met to discuss favorite verses of Scripture. I can't remember the specific passages referenced, so I'll make some up.

The first man said that his most inspiring verse came from the Gospel of John, because it gave him comfort that God would love man so much that He would sacrifice His own Son.

The second man said his favorite scripture was the account of the prodigal son, because it clearly says that man can always return to the Father; it gave him hope.

Finally an old gent stood and said that his very favorite passage of Scripture was: "It came to pass." Then he sat again.

One of the other fellows said, "That doesn't make any sense. What are you trying to say?"

The old man slowly rose from his seat and said, "'It came to pass' occurs throughout the entire Bible more than any other verse. This tells me: It came to pass. Thank God it didn't come to stay!"

I wish I had heard that gem of wisdom while my children were smoking marijuana and drinking alcohol. Some days I just wanted to crawl in a hole and never come out. I wondered if the drug use would destroy us. The '70s twisted our lives every which way.

As soon as Eddy turned eighteen, he was handed a large sum of money which was part of his inheritance from his father's insurance policy.

Money can be useful. It can buy medicine to save lives, food to feed us, heat for our homes. It can give us the things we need. In the hands of young, disturbed boys, money can be a killer. Eddy, Larry, and Steven refused to accept that they were hanging with the wrong crowd. The kids were tough and not their friends at all. In fact, I went so far as to say that they were enemies. My sons became zombies. Their entire personalities changed. Outgoing, fun-loving Eddy became sullen and moody. If he wasn't drunk, he was high. Larry became a wisecracking, smart-mouthed, mixed-up kid. Steven was the saddest of all. He hated school. The teachers called every other day and said, "Come and get your son; he is out of control."

Eddy withdrew so far into himself that I tried to get him some counseling. He refused to open up; wouldn't say a word. I was frightened. I did not know that Frank had actually told Eddy that if Eddy burdened me with his problems, Frank would kill him. It took years before Eddy would tell me about his fears.

I knew that Frank had threatened my life and Eddy's, but I had no way of knowing what he said to the kids when I wasn't around. I wanted to be friends with Frank. He wanted something else. He said if I would come back to him, he would give Eddy back to me after he moved into his mother's house. Cold chills ran up my spine when he said that he had been working on controling Eddy's mind since day one.

Caroline rescued me from despair more times than I can remember. Somehow, she always knew when I felt like banging my head into a wall. I'll never forget one particular night when I lay in bed trembling and weeping, unable to think straight. She called and said, "Girl, I'm here. I'm holding on to your hand. I won't let you go. I will never let you go. I love you, girl. Do you hear me? Are you listening? I love you; God loves you. Your children may spin around the block a few times but they'll come home. They will come home. Believe it. Believe it. Acorns don't fall far from the trees."

Then my dear friend prayed for me. The first thing she did was call down a band of angels to watch over me. If anyone knew me, it was Caroline. And she loved me anyway. She knew there just had to be more than one angel.

I couldn't sleep I was so worried about my children. If I lost them, I wondered what my life would mean. To gain everything else, yet fail as a mother, would be total defeat in my mind. When I thought about all Larry and I had been through together, it nearly broke my heart. Why would God bring me to this place just to see me in utter despair? I needed a band of angels, all right—some to clean the house, some to take care of the bills, some to raise the kids, and some to cut the hair. I wished most of all that some of the angels would give me a real break and get Frank out of my life.

Someone told me about a woman who was supposed to be close to God and could tell you things just by looking at your face. Alice and I were going to see her. The night before we were scheduled to go, I had a vision. No, I was not lit to the gills, and I have never smoked marijuana nor taken hallucinogenic drugs in my life.

Sitting on my bed, about to go to sleep, I looked at my dresser mirror and saw what appeared to be a home movie playing right on the glass. I thought I was cracking up. The image showed a fat lady with blonde hair and me sitting at a round maple table. There was a burning candle on the table, so I could clearly see everything in the room. No matter how hard I rubbed my eyes, the imaged stayed on the mirror until it faded out at least two minutes later.

When Alice heard my story the next day, she said I was imagining things.

"Maybe I had a sign not to go," I said. Alice still wanted to go, so we did.

I am so thankful that I told Alice my vision before we went to the lady's house rather than after. When the door opened, there she was— the fat lady I had seen on my mirror. Alice looked like she had seen a ghost. Her jaw dropped as she said, "Whoa!"

Since I had been in that lady's house the night before through my mirror, I could have taken us directly to the room with the burning candle and round maple table. It was all there as I had seen it.

The lady said, "You have psychic power." Then she informed me that eventually Frank would fade into the sunset. She also told me that my children were a problem. I nearly choked at that. Then she told me that I had to be strong. Was that an unimpressive revelation or what? Every mother has to be strong. Who was she kidding? She was playing it safe with generalities.

"Pray," she said next. "Pray and the angels will help you."

Yes, bands of them, I thought. Caroline had already sent a band of them; how many would I need, for goodness sake?

Alice kept her eyes on me for a long time after that as if I were some sort of "New Age metaphysic." If this was a "gift," I didn't care to have it. I thought it was too spooky to see something on my mirror that happened the next day. I preferred the power to draw in crowds of customers who needed haircuts. Truthfully, though, I did sense that God had been leading me to put no faith in the "insights" of psychics.

On July 12, 1979, soon after my thirty-seventh birthday, Pattie gave birth to Elizabeth Noel Elliott. She was my first grandchild, and her name was the most beautiful name in the world. She had a head full of dark hair, and her skin was lovely and pink. I held her tiny body in my arms and thought about my own grandmother. I determined that I would sing to Elizabeth, and we would find our own special song. She could take baths in my tub full of water, clear up to her neck, and sing her heart out. We would have tea parties and play dress-up. Whispering "I love you" in her ear, I welcomed her into my life.

Pattie and Tony were living in my town house, but Tony had just lost his job with an exterminating company. He couldn't pay the $175.00 monthly mortgage payment, and I couldn't carry them, so they called Tony's parents. They said he could move his family into an old schoolhouse on their property. The building had electricity but no bathroom. Their new dwelling was in a rural area of Virginia that I lovingly referred to as "Cornfield County."

Pattie and Tony had spent every cent of her father's insurance money. She had nothing to show for it after the bank repossessed her new car. I was worried about what would become of my daughter and my only grandchild.

Soon after that happened, Eddy and I got into a horrendous fight. I yelled and screamed like an old fishwife. It was not a pretty sight. I said if he was so smart, he could just leave and fry his brains. I reflected that I had held him in my arms when he was born and thanked God for him.

I had watched him take his first steps and heard him say his first word. I would not watch him kill himself with pot and alcohol.

Eddy was still receiving Social Security benefits and government compensation. There was more than enough to take care of his needs. As long as he stayed in school and maintained passing grades, he'd be fine, financially anyway. Eddy was smart enough to finish high school and said he wanted to go to college. It came to pass that he left home, and we didn't communicate for a very long time.

Edgar "Leon" Tolson, my first love.

Alice Ruth, my mother at age thirty.

"Curley" Hughes (Daddy to me), Golden Gloves
Featherweight Champion the year I was born in 1942.

My grandparents: Ruth Irma and Elias Arthur Place.

Family photo from left to right: Me, Alice Carol, Diane, Daddy, Kathleen and brother Joe.

Thomas "Tom" Campion (the love of my daughter's life)
and Patricia, my little girl all grown up and happy.

Edgar Leon Tolson Jr. and his beautiful bride Kathryn
"Kathie" Childress Tolson (she's a special gift to me too!).

Larry Hughes Tolson, my loving son and inspiration,
one week after his transforming surgery.

Frank Steven Smith III, my son the poet.

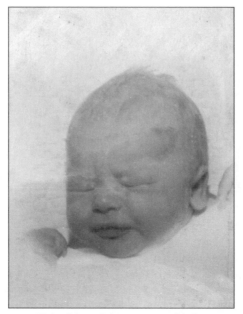

Michael Leon Tolson, my angel baby.

Elizabeth Noel Elliott, "My Sunshine" first
grandchild at age fifteen.

Wesley Aaron Tolson, my grandson, otherwise known as "Wesley the Wonder Boy," and my angel cover girl granddaughter, Sara Elizabeth Tolson.

Twin grandchildren, Katia Marie Locke "Katie," and Marshall Edward Locke "Little Boy Boo."

My "Golden" friend of thirty years, Caroline King Hasberry, and me.

My "Coupon Clipping" husband and his children Commander Edward Stephen Locke
(U. S. Navy ret.) and from left to right top row: Daughter and computer whiz, Debi,
and her husband Bobby. Bottom row: Scott (the best at lawn maintenance and
all-around nice guy), my wonderful daughter in-law, Shirley Craig Locke,
and Steven Timothy Locke, a special friend to me.

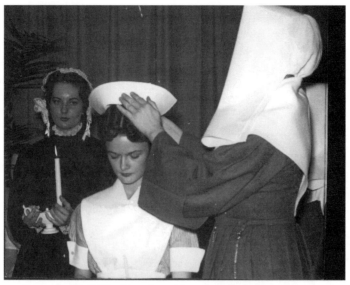

My very "saintly" looking sister Diane, receiving her nurses cap.

Daddy and Grandma Hughes
(and the famous Hughes ears).

CHAPTER 26

The Governor
of New York

My night classes gave me much to look forward to. They got me out of the house and took my mind off my problems. In the fall of 1978, I was working on a research paper on the effects of mass hypnosis in certain religious cults. I had heard of a female religious leader who employed every technique possible to work up a crowd, and I asked my sister if she would attend a session with me. Alice was impressed that I seemed to know what the woman would say and do next. It was one of those nights that we didn't want to end. We were like children giggling in church. Everything was funny. A man sitting next to us held a ten-dollar bill in his left hand and tried to goose me with the other. I scrunched up next to Alice. She moved, I moved, he moved, until we nearly fell into the aisle! Boy, could we pick seats.

The lights flashed, a repetitious drumbeat sounded in the background, and the audience hummed a mantra while swaying to the music. I was extremely proud of myself when I predicted the exact time when the "love" offering would be collected. When they passed the offering plate, the man with ten dollars put in his money and took out eight dollars in change.

On the way home, we stopped at a local pub to discuss the events of the evening and have a glass of wine. Alice looked especially beautiful that night. Everyone in the place seemed to be at least ten years my junior, just about Alice's age. She danced and laughed and had a ball. The area was as familiar to me as the back of my hand. I knew the people and there was no reason to feel concerned for our safety.

Just as I was about to suggest that we leave, I noticed a tall, handsome man stroll up to the bar. When Alice sat down for a breather, I said, "Looky there, Alice, it's Clark Kent." She agreed that he was interesting and returned to the dance floor. After I had consumed some more wine, I motioned for the waiter. I pointed to the tall man, gave the waiter a dollar, and requested that he ask the gentleman if he was over thirty-five with any social class whatsoever. If the answer was affirmative, would he care to join me? My eyes followed the messenger as he approached the stranger, and I watched for a reaction.

I could see that Clark was amused and responsive, but it took him a while to think of something clever to say. He ambled over to our table and casually asked, "Are you the little lady with the request?"

I smiled and nodded.

In true John Wayne style, he said, "Let's just say, I get by." He sat down and asked a few questions of his own, like "What is your name?" "Do you come here all by yourself?" "Aren't you a bit overdressed?" and, of course, "What's a sweet thing like you doing in a place like this?"

I knew he was not prepared for my answers: My name is Billie Smith. I am a master barber and own a shop a few blocks down the street. This is my sister Alice. We just came from church because I was collecting information for a research paper that I am writing for a college project.

He sat quietly and seemed to be deciding if: 1) I was the biggest liar he had ever met in his life; 2) I had consumed too much wine; 3) There was a hidden candid camera somewhere in the place; 4) I was on a leave of absence from a mental institution or heavily medicated; or 5) All of the above.

To bring him back to reality, I asked, "What do you do?"

A sly smile came across his face and he said, "I'm the governor of New York."

We both laughed so hard our sides ached. Then he asked to see my driver's license for proof of my identity.

We talked and laughed for hours. The night had flown by. Alice and I hated to go, but we both had to work the next day. I kissed him good night and said to Alice, "Tomorrow I won't even remember his name. But, he won't ever forget mine."

Two weeks later, I got the shock of my life. As I was closing the shop and leaving for a night class, a tall naval officer walked in the door. I knew it was none other than the "governor" himself. I was so embarrassed my face turned red and my neck blotched. My employees were gawking, so I waltzed him out the door.

There didn't seem to be a graceful way out, so I just told him I was ashamed of myself. The truth was, I did not make a habit of going to bars, and I definitely didn't have a lot of experience picking up men. It was one of those nights when a few glasses of wine had given me courage to do and say things that I wouldn't have said otherwise. What else could I say, except that I was sorry and that I could not get involved with anyone because, as I had mentioned, I was trying to get out of a bad marriage.

Clark, or rather, Ed, looked straight into my eyes, reminded me that he was also getting out of a bad marriage and said he understood completely. Then he added that it had taken him two weeks to get his nerve up, and he didn't want to receive the bum's rush. He said he couldn't remember feeling as comfortable or having as much fun talking with anyone. He said he wasn't interested in a blazing romance either but that it sounded as though we could both use a friend. He would be at the same pub on Thursday night and would like to see me and, of course, Alice, too.

Alice and I went to the pub the following Thursday, and Ed was already there. Again we laughed and carried on half the night. I had never met anyone who was so easy to talk to. It really seemed innocent enough, until about six months later, Ed asked if I ever went anywhere without Alice. I told him I never did. Still, I knew we were both in trouble.

Ed asked me to lunch at a Chinese restaurant. I agreed. Alice and I arrived ahead of time, and she hid in the booth behind my seat. When he saw only me, his face lit up. Then Alice jumped out of her booth and said, "Hi, Ed." He took it good-naturedly, and we all had a good laugh.

Ed had been in the navy since he was nineteen. He was a lieutenant and was what the navy called a "mustang," which means he had worked his way through the enlisted ranks and achieved officer status. He had done what he described as the "right" thing by marrying his expectant girlfriend. They had three children. She was a diagnosed manic-depressive, and their marriage had been over for years. He had had an affair three years or so before meeting me and said that was not the way he wanted to live his life.

One thing was certain, I didn't want to spend my life having affairs, either. I had already been involved with a doctor and still felt guilty long after the whole thing cooled off. My conscience was now bothering me because I knew where things were heading. How could I let myself get into a situation like this? I was still legally a married woman, even though my marriage had been over for a very long time. In the back of my mind, I knew I had to finally stop the madness at home and leave Frank, who didn't want a divorce.

We hadn't slept in the same bed for ages. Frank enjoyed picking things out of the air just to see what hurt me the most. His rampages went on for hours while he paced back and forth and called me names. After hearing the same things for so many years, I knew what he would say next. I thought I couldn't make it without him, though. His verbal attempts to beat me down reached unbelievable, vicious depths not worthy of repeating. Sometimes he went on so long that I thought I would crack. Once I was so distraught that I went into my bathroom and broke everything that was breakable. Sometimes I lost control of myself and cursed and hollered back in self defense.

In the past, in order to protect what sanity I had left, I had to learn to make myself numb. Frank had a scar on his cheek that was in the shape of a star. I stared at that scar and sang a hymn to myself, over and over. After a while, I didn't hear a word he said. When he finished, he stomped off to bed very satisfied with himself that he had really told me a thing or two. For nearly six months before we finally separated, Frank would scream and pace back and forth for hours each night. Then, before he left for work in the morning, he'd come into my room and place a cup of coffee on my nightstand. Then he'd apologize.

I never wished Frank any harm. After all, he had helped me get Larry's eye. He had struggled with me every step of the way through all the surgical procedures so that my son would have a decent life. No matter what happened, I would not forget that. He had loved Larry and he had loved me. I knew that he couldn't help himself. He told me his mother used to lock him in a closet for long periods of time when he was a child.

Finally, Frank moved into his mother's house which was not being used because she was hospitalized. Ema had a complete mental break-down after a brief marriage to a wonderful man. Voices in Ema's head told her to slash her wrists. She cut herself up with a butcher knife. The last time I saw Ema, she cried when she saw me.

"I knew you would come," she said.

I asked if there was anything I could do for her, and she asked me to put some lotion on her legs, which I did. We had a nice visit. Frank was surprised when I told him what she had said. She seldom ever recognized anyone, including Frank. Ema stayed institutionalized until she died. I hope she found the peace of mind that eluded her during her life on earth.

Then Frank started seeing a very young German girl who used to work for me at the Plaza Trail Hairport. I thought that it would cool things down some, but it didn't. He called the shop, not only threaten-ing to kill me, but also claiming he would kill Ed. I was so upset I could hardly sleep. Ed only laughed.

Frank and I went at it tooth and nail for over a year. He wanted me to assume all of the liabilities, while he skipped off with everything of value. Every other week, I received a new proposal. In the end he won, but he lost. In order to retain my home, I had to assume $40,000 of debt owed against the house in addition to the mortgage payment—which was around five-hundred dollars per month—plus give Frank $15,000 in cash, everything in the garage, most of our books, and a twenty-dol-lar gold piece he had given me as a gift. He wanted the promissory note for $10,000 from the couple who had purchased one of our shops, and wanted all the interest in the Holland Road shop, which was the only shop that was really making any money. I got the house, the debt, the townhouse that had very little equity, a losing shop on Plaza Trail that was going downhill fast, and a brand new shop with no clientele and $1,249.50 in rent to be paid monthly. I felt like it was at least a chance, so I accepted his conditions.

When I think about Frank, I don't feel any anger. I'm sure about that. He had more problems than he could deal with—and I had more than my share of problems also. I wish him joy, and I even have a song in my heart for him, "The Bluebird of Happiness." We have a son, and no human being is a mistake. I truly believe it was all a part of some-thing far greater than any mortal is capable of understanding. "And we know that all things work together for good to them that love God, to them who are the called according to his purpose" (Romans 8:28).

My hours at the shop were long and hard, but I longed to get out of the mess I had been in for so long. I related to a verse from a Simon and Garfunkel song in which the singer tells God he is knocking on His door again since He could be trusted. I was knocking on God's door again with another pile of broken dreams and promises that I couldn't keep.

I threw myself on God's mercy. I had a chance, and I was going to give it all I had. Perhaps that light in the distance wasn't a train after all, and maybe this time I just might make it. To be safe, I called down a band of God's angels myself. I asked that they watch over me, and if it wasn't asking too much, that they would send some customers.

As always, my dear friend Caroline was around to tell me that everything was going to be all right. Her telephone calls were my only life line in times of despair. When I was shaking in my boots, and the world looked like it was caving in around me, she knew I was hurting, scared, and feeling alone. Sometimes, when I was so weak that my faith seemed as small as a mustard seed, the spirit within her told her that I needed encouragement. Sweet Caroline told me she was holding my hand; she wouldn't ever let me go. Everything would work together for good. God was still on His throne and He, not man, was in control. God loved my children, and God loved me. She said, "Believe it, girl. Believe it."

CHAPTER 27

That Rat, Ed

E d and I dated on weekends. It was a set thing, I thought. One Friday afternoon he called the shop. He said he would not be picking me up that evening. When I asked why, he said that he just couldn't make it. My remarks were not pleasant.

I said, "Fine, I'll find someone who can take me out."

He said, "Fine, I hope you have a lovely evening."

I said, "Fine, I hope you have a lovely evening."

The gentleman sitting in my chair getting a haircut saw that I was a bit shaken and asked me what had happened. I told him that my Friday night date had just canceled.

He replied, "Good, I've been wanting to ask you out. Will you have dinner with me tonight?"

"Yes, thank you, I would love to have dinner with you." I gave him my address and phone number.

"I'll pick you up at seven-thirty."

Before I left the shop, Ed called. "Well, did you find someone to take you out?"

"I sure did. He was sitting in the chair when you called."

"That's great. What time will you be leaving?" I told him the time. "Well, I hope you have a great time."

Out loud I said, "I will, and I hope you do the same." Inwardly I didn't think nice thoughts.

Garry was right on time. We walked right out to his car, he opened my door, then got in on the driver's side. Just then, Ed pulled up next to the car and sat looking at us.

"Billie, is that someone you know?"

"Well, Garry, I thought I knew him, but I don't think I do at all." I told Garry that it was the date who had stood me up at the last minute. I said, "Please, let's go." We drove off and left Ed parked in front of my house.

We went to a fabulous restaurant. Garry was attentive and very charming. He was a perfect dinner companion. I wasn't about to let Ed ruin my evening. After dinner, Garry asked if I would like to stop by his house for a nightcap. I said that I would be delighted.

His home was in an upscale neighborhood, not far from the Virginia Beach oceanfront. His yacht was tied up alongside a dock in his back-yard. The house was beautifully furnished. Garry told me that he was divorced and had one daughter. He was what many single women would be looking for. At eleven o'clock, I asked him to take me home. He shook my hand at my front door and said he hoped I could work things out with my friend.

No sooner had I pulled on my flannel nightgown and crawled into bed, when I heard scratching at the window. As I looked out, Ed was standing in the grass a few feet from the Echols' house, teetering and talking loud enough to wake up the whole neighborhood.

I didn't know what to do. Jim and Sylvia Echols were the nicest people in the world. They had always been so kind in the face of all the crazy things that went on around my house. They were pillars of the community. Jim was the director of Tidewater Transit. People knew and respected him.

Sylvia was involved with Meals on Wheels, and if she wasn't at home, she was at her church. I once thought that if I could trade places with her I'd have it made. Sylvia had everything that I originally wanted for myself. One husband, a beautiful family, and stability. I loved the good-ness in her. She was so much like my sister Diane: warm, saintly-look-ing, and naturally kind. Both being nurses, they had the caring qualities so vital to that profession.

To me, the Echols family was a prime example of how people should live. I was willing to bet that Jim even said grace when they had no company at the table. Jim and Sylvia did an excellent good job raising their children. Their family life revolved around the church, and their children grew up with values that gave them strength through their turbulent teen years. They never got into trouble the way kids like mine, who came from broken homes, did.

Besides all that, Jim and my brother-in-law Chuck had attended the same university. Jim, Sylvia, Diane, and Chuck frequently saw each other at various university events. I wanted Jim and Sylvia to be able to say, "Billie is doing fantastic. Boy, is she getting her life together. You can be proud of her." My pride still had a firm grip. There I was—the only divorced woman on the cul-de-sac, living right next door to the Cleavers. I was so embarrassed I could've cried. It was midnight, and Ed wasn't singing love songs.

I whispered, "Go home!"

He said, "If you won't let me in, I'll break your window."

I was frantic. Then he reminded me that he had a key to my shop, which I had given him in case of a fire or some other emergency. He lived closer to the shop than I did. I told him to put the key in the mailbox and go home. Again he shouted, and I agreed to open my door.

Dressed in a suit, Ed had confetti in his hair and a button in the shape of a frog on his lapel. He was lit to the gills. He broke into tears and cried, "I can't believe you went out with another man!"

"I can't believe you were so rude that you would break a date with no explanation."

"I can't believe you went out with another man," he said again and left. I looked at the Cleavers' house, grateful that the lights were off.

The next day, Saturday, was the busiest day of the week at work. I didn't have time to worry about that rat, Ed. Garry brought in a cup of coffee and said that he had had a lovely time on our date. I thanked him and told him that I also had enjoyed his company. He asked me to call him if I felt like going out again. Garry was a gentleman.

At six o'clock, my day was almost over. Then Ed strolled in. He asked all my employees to leave and give him some time to redeem himself. They got out as fast as they could. Ed picked me up off of the floor and sat me on the back counter of my workspace. He told me that he had made lieutenant commander the night before. The man officiating the ceremony had been friends with him and his former wife. Even though she had not been invited, he felt that it would have put everyone in an awkward position if I had been there.

Ed made the wrong choice to leave me in the dark, wondering what kind of man he was. He should have trusted me enough to tell me the truth. His decision caused me to rethink our relationship. I thought that maybe we should cool things down. I told him so.

I could tell he was worried. He asked me to marry him. He said that if he lost me because of a stupid mistake, he would be miserable. Truthfully, I was thinking he was pretty miserable already. He asked if he could come to my house and talk that night. I told him that I had things to do. He pressed to find out what was possibly more important than he was.

"I'm having my income taxes done by a man I have known for ages."

"Who would do income taxes on a Saturday night? And what does his wife think of you coming over to work on a weekend?"

"He isn't married."

Ed groaned.

I thought, *Let him stew.*

When I arrived at home, Ed was sitting in my den like a big wounded bird. He said that he wasn't going to be easy to get rid of. Ed asked me to marry him again. He said that he wanted to spend the rest of his life with me. I knew he was running scared. I didn't want to make any more mistakes. I thought God might not continue to bail me out of bad situations. If I refused to learn and use good judgment, what could I expect?

I didn't owe Ed anything. Sometimes I wanted him to disappear. For the first time ever, I had the chance to make decisions based on the right reasons. I wasn't running away from anybody. My security didn't depend on a man. I could work and take care of myself.

Yet I still couldn't tell him to hit the road. I was happy to hear from him. The big lug had an easy way of laughing at the silliest things. And we did have some great times together.

. . . .

CHAPTER 28

A House with
No Walls

I decided I would hang in there with Ed, even though he was sending some selfish signals. Nobody's perfect, I reasoned. We went for a
ride one afternoon. Ed had received a brochure in the mail, adver-
tising property for sale in Bracey, Virginia, on Lake Gaston, and he thought
it would be a nice day out, if nothing else.

That night I had a dream. I was walking through a heavily wooded
area. The brush was so thick I had to shield my eyes from the vines that
were hitting my face. I struggled along until I came to a clearing. I stood
on a sandy little beach and saw the most beautiful body of water surrounded by magnificent old trees. I thought this was a message telling
me that my struggles would soon be over. At last, beauty and serenity
were waiting for me on the other side of the forest.

I packed up a picnic lunch and off we went. When we arrived in
Bracey, we met a real-estate agent named Oliver Chandler who told us
that the owner of the property, Pete Rudd, had been diagnosed with
stomach cancer and that it was terminal. On the advice of his doctor,
he was liquidating his assets. The property for sale was well below
market value.

Yeah, yeah, let's see it, I thought.

I feared Oliver would have a stroke taking us through acres and acres of land. We struggled through thick brush and vines, then found ourselves standing on a small patch of sand. My heart raced when I saw the water and the fine old trees. Ed stood drooling.

We talked about buying it. Ed said he had a five-year plan that this could work into. He wrote a check for half of the deposit, and I wrote a check for the other half. We were landowners.

Every chance we had, we went to the lot. Ed carried on about his five-year plan, and I wondered where all of this was taking me. The townhouse and the Hairport on Plaza Trail sold. I saved every cent I could get. My debt was being reduced. I paid off my car. Two boarders living in my house helped give me a nice little nest egg. The shop was doing well too. My long hours were finally paying off. The situation with Frank was even calming down. Could I dare to think that we were getting past the anger and into a friendship?

An old Chinese proverb says, "Be careful what you wish for; it may come true." It was written for fools like me. It's a brilliant piece of wisdom. Too bad I didn't heed that warning. There were danger signs all around me concerning Ed, but I ignored them. Little things began to surface, like his advice concerning my children. He constantly told me they were headed for trouble. He also said he was worried about my safety. I should change the locks. He pointed out all the things that could happen.

According to Ed, my car was more economical on gas, so we used mine, while his sat in the driveway. My gasoline bills doubled. I made up one excuse after the other for Ed, and considered myself blessed that he was so stable, so nonviolent.

But, Prince Edward had never grown up. He was a spoiled child, used to having his way about everything. I needed the added aggravation like I needed a fingernail on the end of my nose. He whined and complained like an old woman. However, he did laugh and want to go places and do fun things. He took me to Busch Gardens and Seashore State Park.

I started having difficulty handling my son Steven. He was unhappy with me and with himself. He missed his father. They understood each other. He was having so much trouble at home and at school that I was forced to take him to a child psychiatrist twice a week. I couldn't keep up the pace. I decided that I was not doing my son any favors by keeping him. I called Frank and told him that I needed help with our son. He agreed to take Steven to live with him. That may have been a mistake, but whatever Steven needed, he wasn't getting it from me. It was not an easy decision. I knew my son would end up thinking that I just plain didn't want him. That was never the case. I will always love him. To this day, he hasn't gotten over it. There is great sadness in me because I couldn't help him. Considering it all, it was the most difficult thing I have ever experienced.

Larry stayed spaced out most of the time and lay around vegetating. His only exercise was flipping the channel selector for the television. He shifted from pillar to post. The only one whom he thought he could trust was his lifelong friend, Larry Whitbred. They had been in the same class in the seventh grade and had remained friends. Just like my Larry, Larry W., because of his own health problems, could not participate in contact sports or physical education classes. They understood each other and were bonded by the pain they had suffered their entire lives. By the time my Larry graduated from high school, he had access to the insurance money from his father's estate. Larry W. had lost his father too. The two of them were drowning their sorrows in booze and sucking up marijuana like it was going out of style. Larry drifted away from me.

For the first time in my life, I was alone. I was lost and unhappy without my children. What could I do? I wasn't going to watch them die. I threw myself into my work and tried to find out what was going on with my sons. They drifted from Leon's mother's house to Frank's house. Eddy ended up sleeping in the woods with his dog Budweiser after Frank threw him out.

Eddy, Larry, and Larry W. somehow got together to rent a house. I was delighted, hoping they were getting their acts together. The house was near where my children had grown up. It was a nice little three-bedroom place. I gathered all my spare items and filled the house with furniture I bought at garage sales. One of my customers gave me a dining room set for the boys. They were getting along fairly well. The best news of all was that Larry was going to college.

Ed and I spent as much time at the lake as we could, and we started looking at house plans. We found a cute A-frame cottage in a book and a builder who agreed to construct the shell at a reasonable price. We split the cost and the house went up. Every weekend, we hammered, nailed, and smiled at our good fortune. We played music, danced, and laughed together in our house with no walls. We slept on lawn furniture and bathed on rafts in the lake. Eventually our cabin on Lake Gaston was complete.

We drove to Virgilina, Virginia, to pick up my granddaughter, one hour's drive from our lake house. Ed didn't say too much while I bubbled with thoughts of being with her for the weekend. He acted childish and moody during our visit. He resented the attention that I gave her and wouldn't even watch her playing in the water while I prepared some lunch. How anyone could be jealous over a child was beyond me.

About this time, Ed received orders to the USS *Guadalcanal*. First we drove to Elizabeth City, North Carolina in July 1982, and were married. I thought it was a big mistake, but I would not admit it. No one knew of our marriage, and Ed did not want anyone to know. We spent our wedding night at the lake. I stayed awake late, asking myself why I had agreed to such a marriage so soon after getting out of a nightmare? This was the only time I had ever had a chance to make a right choice. Had I messed up again? If I had, it was my own fault. I was forty years old and still not very smart.

Ed shipped out, and I wrote him faithfully. He sent me a few letters but said he wasn't a writer. Meanwhile, I found out there were plenty of interesting things that I could enjoy by myself.

My shop was doing well. I had a deal with a Campbell's soup salesman: two bags of dented cans of food for one haircut. I enjoyed soup, beans, and all kinds of juice. I closed off most of the rooms in my house after the boarders left. I lived in the kitchen and den. I saved my money and paid off every single cent of my debts. Then I sold my business. I had a written agreement with the new owner that I could still work there and pay a ridiculously low amount of rent for my chair space. The best part was that I could leave whenever I felt like it.

During most of my spare time, I thought about how I wanted to spend the rest of my life. If necessary, I'd buy another shop and start out fresh with no bills hanging over my head. I rehearsed everything I was going to say to Ed when he came home.

Naturally, he was happy to see me. Ed was even agreeable to a long talk about our future. I told him that things were going to have to change or we had no marriage. Since he didn't want my family around, I suggested that he could visit his children at their homes the way I visited mine.

Lieutenant Commander Locke was not thrilled over what I proposed, nor was he happy about my decision to sell my business and pay off all of my debts without consulting with him first. He was used to calling the shots and telling others what to do.

Round two with the big Polish prince and the little Irish Colleen was going to be very interesting. I almost felt sorry for him. He hadn't realized that he had married a woman who would be difficult to control. Maybe impossible would be more accurate. That defiant child inside of me was raring to go. Daddy would have been proud of my resolve. If nothing else, I would drive Ed to drink or to church; it was his choice. I just knew there was something good inside of Ed.

I had choices too. I could allow him to get the best of me, or I could teach him a thing or two.

Ed smelled challenge in the wind.

CHAPTER 29

The Polish Prince

A s much as I cared about Ed, I didn't notice the symptoms of a
man who had been the center of everyone's attentions all his
life. When he opened his mouth after birth, he screamed and got
the attention he desired. As he grew up, his methods varied, but his goals
and results remained self-centered. I didn't see any of this in our early
years. We were too busy having fun.

When Ed's grandparents had come to this country, Polish immigrants
were typically labeled as stupid. All brawn, no brains. They couldn't
read English, but they knew how to work. Most of the men took jobs in
factories or coal mines. Ed's grandmother scrubbed floors in an office
building. They both worked hard to give their daughters "the good life"
in America. They owned their own home in less time than it took most
people to dream of such a luxury.

Sarah, Ed's mother, was a saint. Her little Edward was the first male
grandchild in the family and grew up in his grandparents' home. If he
couldn't get what he wanted from his mother, he went to see Babci, his
grandmother. She would give it to him. She adored her little Edjiu, her
Polish Prince. Get the picture?

Aunt Martha (his mother's sister) also lived in the same home. She
adored little Ed. Prince Edward had three women at his beck and call,

three women whose sole purpose in life was serving their darling boy. It stayed that way until he was eighteen when his only sibling, David, was born, the change-of-life baby and answer to his mother's prayers for someone else to love. Little Dave was also his father's pride and new baseball buddy.

Steve, Ed's father, was Ukrainian and came from a family of ten children. Magda, Steve's mother, had two other children who had died and several who were stillborn. His father, Andrew, was a factory worker with principles. He had refused to cross a picket line and had lost his job. He then sold the family home and moved them to a farm during the Great Depression. There was too much competition and times were harsh. No matter how hard Andrew struggled, he sank deeper in debt. His older children tried to help by working, but they were unable to compete. When Andrew couldn't make ends meet, he saw his failure as a judgment from God. He left the church that he had helped to build and never returned. Then he went into the bootleg whiskey business.

I tried to understand Ed by learning about his family, especially his father. I was privileged to know Steve's inner self after I married his son. Steve had seen Andrew beat his wife, lose his self-respect, and kill himself drinking too much. During the beatings, Steve often diverted his father, who then chased and threw things at him until he passed out. Steve grew up using his wits and manipulative skills that he learned trying to survive the harshness of his childhood. They had no terms for dysfunctional families in those days.

Because of the childhood I had experienced, I was able to soothe the child in Steve. I understood him. In my mind's eye, I saw him running, running, trying to escape, trying not to hear the vulgar cursing and vicious remarks of his drunken father. He eventually hid in the barn and waited for his mother. Magda always came with food. She didn't speak. What could she say? How could she thank him?

Before his father gave up on himself, Steve had once taken violin lessons. His dream in life was to become a lawyer. He left home as soon as he could but had nowhere to go. As a vagrant, his bed, more often than not, was a park bench or the ground under a bridge.

Steve tried not to be angry, but his frustration surfaced in other ways. He loved Sarah, but he was not a good husband. She busied herself with her little Polish prince, and she relied on her parents for the love and support she needed.

I think Steve looked like Cary Grant. At one time he owned a neighborhood bar and grill in Syracuse, New York, with two of his brothers. The New Spot Grill was a busy place. Everybody knew the Locke brothers. Steve had plenty of friends of both sexes. But really, Steve was a man's man—one of the boys, good old Steve. His main delight in life was beating the system. He watered down the booze and kept two sets of books. He ran parlays on the side for extra cash. He managed to fall and hurt himself and capitalize on circumstances. He was brilliantly cunning.

He did love his family, but Steve really lived for baseball. When Ed was a boy, the relationship he had with his father revolved around "The Baseball Game." Steve taught Ed how to sneak into the parks without paying and rewarded him accordingly. They stood together with their hands on their hearts and sang our national anthem. The love between Ed and his father came together in their mutual enjoyment of sports. Every victory for the home team was a victory for them.

Steve didn't think Ed's first wife Cornelia, or "Corky," was good enough for his son. Steve believed that she came from the wrong side of the tracks and that she had trapped him. She just wasn't up to the standard Steve held for Ed. When the "prince" dropped out of college, his father said it must have been her fault. Steve only spoke to her when spoken to, after Ed did the "right" thing and married her. The entire marriage was rocky. Steve refused to accept her, and she couldn't do anything to win his love. To Steve, she was merely the mother of his grandchildren.

I first met Steve just prior to Ed's daughter Debi's wedding. He was a widower by then. Considering Steve's attitudes towards Corky, I gave our meeting extensive thought and insisted that Steve meet me on my turf. Ed brought his father into the Hairport on a very busy day, which would show Steve that I wasn't starving. Steve could, and would, size up the situation. He would see for himself that I was not somebody who had come in from the rain looking for a meal ticket. Armed with just enough information, I had a plan. First, I would give him a free shampoo and haircut.

He was putty in my hands. The shampoo was perfect. *Stand close . . . rub those temples . . . not too much . . . not too close*, I coached myself. His eyes spun in the back of his head.

"My goodness, it is so nice to meet you, Steve. Ed can't say enough wonderful things about his father. Did you know you could be a Cary Grant look-alike? Now I see where Ed gets his charm and good looks. I do hope that you can join me this evening for some refreshments and Southern hospitality."

My house looked beautiful. In a nice area of town, it was certainly in keeping with Ed's officer status. I served him the best beer, his personal favorite. He loved the oysters and little rolled meat sandwiches. I even sat on the floor at Steve's feet, not dreaming of usurping his rightful place as the dominant male. He didn't know it, but I had him right where I wanted him.

Ed could not believe his eyes. He had warned me that his father was a difficult old cuss who hadn't accepted wife number one. Yet Mr. Sweetheart was smiling and laughing and enjoying my Southern style. He commented that my blonde hair and blue eyes were dazzling and asked where I had gotten the idea of becoming a barber.

Late in the evening, Steve had one more story to tell me, but Ed said they had to leave. He dragged his father out in the early morning hours. His father had stolen all the attention and that was definitely a new experience for Ed. Steve hugged me, kissed me, and said he couldn't wait to see me again. I stood at the door blowing little kisses. "Y'all come back now, you he-ah." After they left, I hummed and sang as I cleaned up. Preparing for bed, I winked at myself in the mirror.

Ed was delighted. He had his father's approval. My father liked Ed too. They also shared a love for baseball. Mama complemented that Ed had an easy way of laughing. He did have a great sense of humor. Why wouldn't he? Everything was going his way. If I pleased his father, I would make them both happy, and Ed did enjoy being happy.

I figured I was pretty clever to win Steve on the first try. Maybe my limited knowledge of psychology was detrimental and I had outsmarted myself. All Ed's background information should have alerted me. If acorns don't fall far from the trees, I was in trouble. Steve was one sharp cookie, and he played the game well.

Having someone around who was responsible, successful, and rational clouded every other issue. How we laughed in those early days. Everything was amusing, and I hadn't known joy in years. I couldn't imagine enough ways to show Ed how glad I was that he was sane, outgoing, and fun. I wanted to give, because that's what love does, it gives.

The problem was Ed knew how to take, but he didn't know how to give. Love to him was: What are you going to do for me today?

CHAPTER 30

Tie Me Kangaroo Down

Just as I was about to sing a goodbye song to Ed, he wanted to talk. Ed admitted that he was a rascal, a wolf in sheep's clothing, and a snake in the grass.

I agreed.

"But," he said, "I love you. I am sorry, and I want to make it up to you." He went on to promise that never again would he try to control me or tell me how to think. He had a five-year plan of self-improvement that was sure to change our lives.

I wasn't forgetting Ed's Ukrainian heritage and the infamous Soviet five-year plans. However, I believed that everybody deserves a second chance. He asked if I would consider a tour of duty overseas. Shortly after his emotional declaration, we left for Australia and a whole new life Down Under.

We moved into a tiny house on the Royal Australian Naval Base in Nowra, which is in New South Wales. Ed received that assignment by virtue of his expertise in repair and maintenance of helicopters. The Australians had recently changed over their naval air force from fixed-wing aircraft soley to helicopters.

After being in Australia several weeks, I was already incredibly bored. Our neighbors were young people who were just starting out, and we were close to retirement age. Ed was replacing Commander Charlie Akins who introduced us to an American officer David Blake and his wife Sarah Jane. David taught at the Royal Australian Naval College at Creswell on Jarvis Bay, which was the Australian equivalent of our Naval Academy.

One day, Sarah told me that the college was in desperate need of a barber for the midshipmen. I was interested. Sarah, or S. J. as she liked to be called, arranged to give a dinner party. She invited the commodore of the college and placed my chair right next to his. While we chatted through dinner, she casually mentioned that I was a master barber.

The commodore said, "I can't guarantee that you will get the job at the college, but if you will send me a letter stating your qualifications, you will be considered."

I got the job. To be perfectly honest, no one else applied.

Going to work that first day, driving on the opposite side of the road, was a blooming nightmare. My car had been sent over with our belongings. Of course, the steering wheel was on the left side with an alarming view of the curb and the ditch beyond. If that wasn't bad enough, when I pulled the sun visor down to shield my eyes from the blazing Australian sun, a humongous tarantula fell on my wrist. That monstrous thing was so big, its hairy legs hung down the sides of my arm. When I shook my hand toward the window, the creepy crawler was so heavy, it made a thumping sound on the window.

Thank God I had sense enough to pull off the road and jump out. I blubbered and screamed on the roadside. I was not getting back in the car with that spider. My screaming got the attention of a passing motorist. He didn't have time to stay, but he offered some encouragement. He said tarantula bites would only make me a bit *crook*, which means "sick," but they wouldn't kill me. Why didn't I feel better?

Next I flagged down a trucker. Truckers weren't afraid of anything. A young man in a bush hat came to my rescue.

He said, "Ah, g'day. 'Avin' a bit o' trouble with the buggy ah we?"

I could barely point to my arm and made wild gestures and guttural sounds.

"Ah, yea, spida. No worries," he said, smiling.

He took my car apart and killed the bloody thing with my hairbrush. Parting, he said, "Ah, g'day, ma'am, and 'ave a bonza go of it."

I stood watching him get back in his truck. After I regained my composure, I was able to sit back in my seat. While I assessed the damage done to my eye make-up, he came back.

He opened the door, put his arms around me, and said, "I reckon the rest of your day has to be much betta now, Love. And if you don't mind me sayin' so, ah'd sorta close your windows from now on. Spidas like to hide in cahs to keep out of the sun and the rain."

The dragon had been slain.

My nearly two years at the college as the official barber was a unique experience. That job made it possible for us to live on the economy and afford to travel all over Australia. We took a cruise to the Fiji Islands. We saw New Zealand, Hong Kong, Singapore, and New French Caledonia, where we might have starved to death if Ed hadn't been able to order chicken and potatoes from the menu by remembering some basic high-school French. A Frenchman seated at a table beside ours was eating raw meat topped with an uncooked egg. Ed never looked better when our cooked meal arrived.

The biggest thrill of all was finding out that I am a flag-waving, anthem-singing American, and proud of it. When Ed and I were invited to social functions, they played our national anthem as our names were announced and we strolled in the door. Chills went up and down my spine hearing the music of our beautiful, treasured "Star Spangled Banner." Ah, the land of the free and the home of the brave!

Australia has the ten most deadly snakes in the world, as well as the most deadly spiders. Funnel Web spiders are very aggressive little buggers who will jump and attack. The Red Back spider is also a killer. Our flowerbeds went to pot because I never did any gardening. One must watch where one sits "down unda." At two o'clock one morning, I nearly sat on a three-toed tree frog that was peering at me from inside the toilet. My screams woke Ed, who tried to flush the frog but couldn't because it kept swimming back. Froggy made queer honking noises and landed on the floor after hitting the wall on Ed's first attempt to grab the slimy devil. My hero finally captured the frog in an empty toilet paper roll and flipped it outside.

The favorite leisure activity of the typical Aussie family is the *barby*, which is grilling *snags* (sausages), burgers, and fried onions. Children relish vegemite (a yeast extract) sandwiches. Vegemite looks like a thick, gooey, dark brown paste. The children grow up on it.

Going on holiday is the national pastime for Australians. They load up the *boot* (trunk) of the car, and off they go. Ayer's Rock is the most popular spot to visit. After driving for days and days on roads that jar the senses, they arrive to view the world's largest monolith. They walk around and around taking photos, have a bit of *tucker* (food), make a few comments, buy a packet or two of souvenir matches or a tea towel, then get back into their cars and drive for days and days to get back home. Then they relive each thrilling moment, showing off pictures or slides.

Now if you have seen the monolith, you can't possibly leave Australia without seeing the world famous "Dog on the Tucker Box." There is some controversy over where the actual event took place. According to one bit of folklore, it was five miles from Gundagai. Another legend says it was nine miles. Whichever mileage you prefer to acknowledge is acceptable to all Australians. One account says, the master who owned the pooch was a *bullocky* (the Aussie equivalent of mule team driver) searching for help. Another story has him as a pioneer in search of water. Either story has him searching in the outback. This one fact is a given: There was a loyal, devoted dog who died guarding a "tucker" (food) box, forever bound to serving his beloved master. When the said master returned and saw the ever faithful watchdog's bones, he was so moved that he erected a monument in Fido's honor. We have a large, beautifully decorated box of matches *and* a tea towel from that stirring pilgrimage.

Sydney is the place to be on Saturday night. Down at the Rocks, Irish music can be heard throughout the city. The favorite local instrument of choice is a *lagerphone,* a piece of wood shaped like a tambourine, tacked with bottle caps, and nailed to a stick. The "lagerphone" is pounded on the floor to achieve the desired rattling sound.

During WWII the Japanese troops were taking over all territory in the South Pacific. The US involvement deterred the Japanese aggression and prevented the continued southward march, which eventually would have reached the northern coast of Australia.

Older Australians remember that they might have been speaking Japanese if it were not for the Americans. They treated us like royalty. We were easily recognized as being from the US, since our car had a big Left Hand Drive sign in the back window and a Virginia license plate. Everywhere we went, folks stopped for a talk. We always were served more "tucker" than the regulars in many places. I don't know how, but restauranteurs spotted us in our car before we walked in the door.

An older couple we met in Queensland invited us to their home for a weekend and wouldn't take no for an answer. They even paid our bus fare back to the hotel where we were staying. Dorie and Dennis Harrington lived not far from us in Kiama, which is one of the most beautiful places in Australia. They had a "barby" for us and invited everyone in their family to come and meet "the Yanks." As I talked, a small boy inched closer and closer to me, trying to touch my skin. I startled him by asking, "What cha doing mate?" He quickly drew back his hand with tears in his eyes. He confessed that he had heard on the "telly" that Americans were cold-blooded, and he wanted to see for himself.

I hugged him. "Son, I'm not cold-blooded. I'm human just like you are. I have children and a granddaughter named Elizabeth, who is your age. I laugh, cry, bleed, and have birthdays just the same as everyone else."

He was so relieved. I was moved and presented with a new realization. For the first time in my life, I was faced with the fact that other countries are not always pro-American. I became acutely aware that as a representative of our nation, my presence would have an impact on small boys as well as on ordinary citizens.

After we cleared the picnic area and brought everything back inside, Dorie wouldn't allow me to help wash dishes. She said that I was a "lady," the first one to ever visit her home, and she would not have it. She wanted to take care of me. God bless that sweet humble soul who thought that I was special. I told her that she was just as fine a lady as I had ever met and she should never let anyone tell her differently.

One week before I left to go home, Dorie called from a hospital and asked if we would come to have dinner and see her at her home before she died. She had terminal cancer and was given six months to live. Ed and I arrived half an hour late because we were making arrangements to have our household furnishings packed. Dorie had insisted that her family wait for their dinner until we got there. The best of everything she had was on display—her finest dishes and her best flatware, which shined on the table that was set just for us. It was extremely difficult to swallow the special meal that had been prepared by the loving hands of a dear friend.

My all-time, most memorable moment came when Ed and I represented our country at the seventy-fifth anniversary of the Royal Australian Navy. Commander and Mrs. Edward S. Locke were formally invited by the United States Embassy to attend a celebration onboard the Mighty Missouri, which was docked at Sydney Harbor. Our famed battleship dwarfed every other ship there, so we had no trouble finding her. An impeccably dressed United States Marine greeted us at the base of the gangway and relayed our names via walkie-talkie to the marine waiting to present us onboard. Because Ed had recently been promoted to the rank of commander, hearing that was extra special. Surrounded by dignitaries from all over the world, we toasted the Australians with champagne that was served for the very first time on a US naval vessel in approximately fifty years. After the commemorative speeches, we sampled shrimp that were hanging in tiers from silver serving trays, finger sandwiches, and delicate little teacakes.

When Ed briefed me for our duty in Australia, he said there were a few things I needed to know. Most importantly, I should keep my mouth shut when it came to politics and religion. We would be hobnobbing with the elite and beautiful people of the world. I could handle that, no worries. Some of the embassy parties were just incredible. Regal, very important people stood around just like every day folks. They formed small clusters and discussed everything . . . from religion to politics. Try as I did, at one particular celebration, I couldn't contain myself and jumped in with both feet. One of the dignitaries looked me up and down and said that I was *cheeky*. I was shocked that a dignitary would actually mention my "behind" in conversation.

I found Ed. "You'll never believe what that man over there said to me." I told Ed about the rear end remark. Well, the food in Ed's mouth nearly flew out as he gasped and sputtered with laughter. After he composed himself, he said that *cheeky* meant I was opinionated.

"I knew that," I said.

I decided to stick to safer topics for the rest of the evening. I was introduced to a German duchess who called me William. Before I opened my mouth, she asked that I dispense with the outdated royal greeting. She said that she liked me—just like that, without mincing words. She was cordial and down to earth. I liked her too. Here hobby was collecting mocca cups. The duchess asked if I had seen anything in the area worth her consideration. We had a grand time talking about antique shops and various sizes and designs of cups.

As part of the Australian community, we discovered the joys of auctions and antique shops. The old player piano that graces our living room came from a small music store in Nowra. When we made the purchase, my picture appeared in the local paper with the pianola, as though I had celebrity status.

Our home is filled with memories of the Edwards family who owned a shop in Berry. When we became friends, they often closed their doors to regular customers while we shared many lunches and happy times. They gave me my pick of anything in the store as a going-away gift.

Ed and I met some wonderful people in those two years, 1984–86. The Clarke family, who refer to themselves as the Griswolds, Garry and Sheryn, live in Washington, DC, now on a two-year tour of duty at the Australian Embassy. They were our newlywed neighbors living next door to us in military housing (or "the patch" as the Aussie's called it). We had some terrific times with them. They were so in love and called each other "darling." They were eager to start their family and overjoyed when Sheryn announced that a baby was on the way. Garry was a handsome young officer. He had the zeal and enthusiasm that marks a true patriot. Sheryn is beautiful and exudes sweetness. When we were invited to tea at her house, she fussed with the preparations all day. She even dipped strawberries in chocolate. It was a lovely added touch. Sheryn was seven months pregnant with her first child when I left.

Now there are two Griswold children. Melissa Noel, the firstborn, is beautiful, bright, and sure to be a success at whatever she chooses to do with her life. She is a gifted writer and artist. Melissa is writing a mystery story and painting lovely floral designs. Personally, I think Melissa is an actress. I know star quality when I see it. Lachlan Alexander is sensitive and loves to read. He would make an excellent prime minister for Australia. He has a tremendous capacity to love all people. He is going to buy a self-contained recreational vehicle for me someday. Lachlan will also design and build an eleven-story house for his mum and dad for their twilight years.

We celebrated Thanksgiving with our friends recently. We held hands around our dining table and prayed. Each person gave individual thanks. The Australians thanked God for our friendship and the opportunity of being with us for a uniquely American experience.

Several of the couples we met in Australia have visited us in Virginia. We cherish each and every moment of their friendship. Our Christmas cards keep us current on the lives of some very special Aussies.

I am blessed to have lived in such a beautiful country. I miss the brightly colored birds: the rosellas, sulphur-crested, and pink cockatoos; lorikeets, the galahs; and—who could forget—the laughing kookaburra. In Green Patch Park, near Jarvis Bay, you can actually hold the crimson rosellas. Some Aussies told us to put seeds in our hands and stand under the trees. I was as giddy as a child when the birds swooped down and landed all over me. Those wonderful tiny creatures ate from my hands.

I have never seen sand as white or beaches as vast as those in Australia. The magnificent sea colors range from the bluest blue to the deepest turquoise.

Everywhere we went, there was something wonderful to see, like the world-class Sydney Opera House where one evening I engaged myself in a conversation with two widows: Olive Dunk and Alcyone Deacon. These dear Australian treasures picked up Ed and me at our hotel the next morning and gave us a guided tour of their city. Our luncheon was served from the "boot" of their car on silver trays. Our new friends had stayed up half the night preparing a feast fit for royalty. We had a beautiful view of Botany Bay to feast our eyes upon while we dined on a blanket underneath grand old eucalyptus trees.

The flaming colors of the sun setting over the Indian Ocean were awe inspiring. We have never seen a more magnificent sunset as the one we saw in the little town of Bunbury. Ed and I huddled together on the beach and watched in amazement. We wished that we could hold back the hands of time and keep the beauty of that magic moment a little longer.

My work as a barber was quite fulfilling too. When I first arrived at The Royal Australian Naval College, the lads enjoyed teasing me over the America's Cup race that America had recently lost to Australia. It was the first time in the history of the race—a hundred and thirty-some years—that the cup had been taken to another country. My remarks made them all laugh.

I said, "Yes, you certainly did win the cup, lads, but you didn't get the saucer. It stays with us forever. We'll die before we give it up."

When they came to trust me with romantic and personal problems, I was honored. It was endearing to think they valued my opinion and would consider my advice. When they cared enough to call me "mum," it touched me deeply.

CHAPTER 31

Back in the USA

Returning to the States meant a lot of catching-up with my children. Eddy had been in and out of trouble. He was hardheaded, like his mother. I hated seeing him depressed, but I couldn't get him to open up. Every time I tried to talk with him, he gave me a flat-line gaze that said, "I'm here, but I'm not listening." I saw myself in those eyes.

His friends were a clever bunch of thugs. In no time at all, Eddy had gone through all the money his father had left him. He dropped out of school and was living hand to mouth.

I went to see him one day, determined to reach him. I said, "Son, you are in a deep pit and you have two choices. One, you can stay there and end up dead, or you can get out and live. It's up to you. You are the master of your own destiny at this point. Everything you really need is already right inside you. All I can do is pray for you."

The next time I heard from Eddy, he asked for money. He promised he was getting his act together. He said he could get out of trouble if I would lend him what he needed. He explained that he wanted to buy a large truck to carry his tools, to pick up heavy equipment, and to transport his new employees. He was going into business for himself.

I loaned him fifteen hundred dollars, and he left town on the run.

I kept hoping and praying for Eddy's genuine turnaround and kept clinging to my sweet memories of him as a child.

When Eddy was five, he fell madly in love with me. He'd peep his little face around corners and blow me kisses in the wind. He also left love notes on my pillow before he could spell *mother*. According to him, his "mouther" could do anything.

Diane was crazy about Eddy and once took him to her home, intending to keep him for a week. She brought him back after a few days because he missed me and was crying. Glowing, I thought my heart would burst; my Eddy wasn't happy without his "mouther."

All my mental pictures of Eddy showed his front tooth missing. He had lost the tooth by falling off of a garbage can. As a knight in shining armor, he was always slaying dragons and protecting us from monsters. The garbage can served as a lookout while he stood tall, guarding the castle.

My memories were a link to the bond that I prayed would keep us from completely losing each other. We were both still weak from all the years of struggling from one day to the next and from being battered and bruised. I knew I had also often failed as a mother. Many nights I cried myself to sleep hoping those beautiful memories of Eddy would take us to better days. The love that had once been so important to a little freckle-faced boy had to mean more than just wishful thinking. Then I would be reunited with my knight in shining armor.

When I arrived back in the States, Larry was renting a room in a private home. Mr. and Mrs. Hurd were fond of Larry, but there was a limit to what they could do for him. He was working at a neighborhood restaurant, making minimum wage. The owner sometimes slipped him an extra twenty for working overtime. He chopped vegetables for "happy hour" and cleaned up the place.

His friend Larry Whitbred had moved to the mountains in Harrisonburg, Virginia. The state had sent him to a rehabilitation program. Larry W. was working at that time at a turkey processing plant. He didn't forget my son and came back to the Virginia Beach area to talk to him. He said life in the mountains was better. The people were kinder and gentler, and told my son that he was on a one-way street leading to nowhere. Larry W. offered to get my Larry a job so he could establish himself in Harrisonburg.

Larry asked my opinion. I said, "Son, you can always come back. If you don't go, you may miss a golden opportunity. Your friend is trying to help you. The two of you have been friends for a long time. Maybe this is the best thing that could happen to you. What do you have to lose?"

Being painfully honest, Larry admitted that he was terribly unhappy. He was dispirited, stumbling around, and getting deeper in debt. He had dropped out of college and didn't know what he was going to do from one day to the next. He was weary of the rat race.

Larry W. came from the mountains to help my son pack up his worldly goods in a small trailer, then off they went. At first, Larry lived with Larry W. and his wife, Patsy, while he got adjusted to his new surroundings. He got a job at the plant with his longtime friend and started putting down some roots. However, all was not well yet.

When he wasn't working, he was drinking by himself in the dark, sinking into a depressing pit. If anyone had a right to feel sorry for himself, it was Larry, but it couldn't continue. He would die.

I cried out in prayer for Larry and spent as much time with him as I could. We patched up the holes in our hearts and found comfort. We had some lovely, tender moments together. I was able to explain many things to soothe him. We leaned upon each other, and our love grew into a larger-than-life love that goes beyond earthly caring.

We stayed in constant contact and discovered how much we have in common. A mother and son were reunited in the sweet communion of our souls. I rejoiced and thanked God for His mercy. Larry gained strength and was able to see and admit to himself that he needed help. He finally got sick of his own pity party. The time was right for Larry to surrender to the healing power of his Heavenly Father. He had to yield, just as we all must acquiesce if we wish to be made whole.

My sweet little "cookie boy" became a man. He admitted himself into a rehabilitation hospital, and life began anew for him. His head cleared. Larry reached out and God was there. He had been waiting.

Nothing in the world had prepared me for the events of the next year. The most frightening discovery was seeing for myself just how damaged my daughter Pattie was from her dysfunctional past.

Like her mother, Pattie didn't get much of a healthy base upon which to build her life. Nothing had been easy for her, and she was so wounded. My daughter's marriage to Tony had been over for several years. She had left their child Elizabeth in the care of Tony and his parents, Sallie and T.C. Elliott, and moved to Michigan.

I didn't hear from her very often and when she did call she sounded so down. Pattie didn't think Tom, her boyfriend, loved her. I didn't know what I could do for her except listen and pray. I suggested she come to Virginia Beach for her vacation that year. Her friend Tom dropped her off and continued on to see his sister in North Carolina.

At the time, I was managing a barber shop on a small army base at Fort Story. I was worried about my daughter and wondering what she would do all day while I was working.

The Fourth of July was coming up, and I decided to have a picnic to celebrate. Included among my several guests was a single man, a chief petty officer who was one of my customers from the barber shop. He and Pattie really hit it off, and she accepted his invitation for a date later.

The next thing I knew, she moved into his townhouse with Elizabeth, who had come for a visit. When I went to see her, I nearly fainted. She was wearing a diamond engagement ring and saying that she was going to be married as soon as possible.

When Tom called to speak to Pattie, I had to tell him that she wasn't there. He left Pattie's car at the Norfolk Regional Airport and returned to his home. Pattie drove back to Michigan, gave her notice at her job, and returned to Virginia Beach with all of her belongings.

In a matter of weeks, Pattie was married and on her honeymoon.

Ten days later, the marriage was over. I loaned Pattie the money to return to Michigan, and she left.

Elizabeth was picked up several days later by her father.

. . . .

CHAPTER 32

A Healing of
the Heart

Ed was still on active duty and stationed in Norfolk. The first mistake I made upon our return to the States was allowing Ed to strong-arm me into a house that I did not like. We still owned the cabin on Lake Gaston, but this new home would be our primary residence. Ed said he would do anything to make it cozy, but it couldn't be done. The master bedroom vent, directly above my head, blew cold air on my face every night. The floors were cold. I don't care what anyone says; heat pumps do not warm air. Homes built on concrete slabs, like ours, have cold floors. Also, the view from our front window was a row of homes exactly like ours but with doors that were different colors. The only trees in the development were in our backyard. The front of our house was mostly garage, which had absolutely no character. To be truthful, I just didn't like the house.

After two years of complaining, Ed was worn down. He found a lot on the Lynnhaven River. I found an English Tudor-style house that we both liked. To prepare for the job ahead, Ed took a course at Old Dominion University on "How to be Your Own Contractor."

The house was put on the market for rent, and we moved out. We moved our household effects into the garage of my old house. Three bachelors who didn't want to leave were renting the house. Ed agreed that they could stay and that we would stay in the finished attic.

Then we took a long vacation with our Australian friends Yvonne and Paul Tribel. Paul, a commander also, had been transferred to HMAS Albatross shortly before Ed and I left Australia. We had really hit it off as if we had known each other for years.

Ed had planned a super vacation for us all. For seven weeks we traveled up the East Coast of the United States, sometimes sharing very close quarters. Yvonne and I were able to communicate on the deepest level. We shared our innermost feelings and got along beautifully.

Paul Tribel cheats at cards, but we got wise to him. We spent hours playing cards in the evenings after sightseeing all day. Ed and Yvonne were both stubborn. They'd sit for hours, long after Paul and I had played out. Yvonne called Ed every kind of awful man for his wily ways, and we laughed good-naturedly until we cried at her frustration.

Our trip ended at our house on Lake Gaston, where the Tribels marveled at how much land and trees there are in the States. They also got the biggest kick out of lightning bugs! We enjoyed watching them delight in this new experience.

Shortly after our trip, we received a disturbing message. In April 1990, Ed's father was hospitalized after suffering a stroke. The news about Steve nearly devastated us. All our plans included him; he was so important to us. I truly loved him as though he were my own father. We were so tuned in to each other that I sometimes knew what he would say before he said it.

My pet name for him was Papa Smurf. Like the cartoon character, Steve loved telling stories with his family and friends gathered around. He also had little gems of wisdom and advice for anyone who cared to listen. I also called him Dear Heart, which he thought was wonderful.

Dear Heart lived in upstate New York, a ten-hour drive from Virginia Beach. Ed had recently retired from the navy, and we had begun to build our dream home. We were up to our ears in details, but we decided that I would care for Steve in Syracuse following his rehabilitation.

Steve was a proud, independent man. It was difficult to convince him that he needed therapy. With going home as his goal, he slowly regained his speech and struggled with basic skills, such as writing his name. Ed and I were moved to tears when Dear Heart showed us his name, which he had painstakingly scrawled across green, lined paper. He grinned like a young boy, eagerly awaiting our approval. Ed shared with me that it took him back to his own childhood, when he had rushed home from school with his name written on the same kind of paper, hoping to impress his father. Roles had reversed, and it was not easy for Ed to handle the mixed emotions.

After three months of therapy, we were able to take Dear Heart back to the home he loved. He never regained full use of his legs but could make transfers from his wheelchair and walk short distances with assistance. We rearranged the house to accommodate Steve's special needs, and he was as happy as he could be under the circumstances.

Every day wasn't peaches and cream with Papa Smurf. Sometimes he wallowed in self-pity, just as anyone might in his situation. He wasn't always easy to please either. Ed and I laugh about one particular occasion. Steve complained incessantly over his special diet for diabetes. According to him, the portions were too large, there were too many meals, he hated skim milk, and nothing had any real taste. On and on he droned, until I came up with what I thought was a perfect way to end the grumbling. I'll never forget the satisfied smile he gave me when I served the same portions of food on the largest plate I could find.

He said, "Well, it's about time you listened to me." The only difference was the size of the dish. I had outfoxed the old fox.

Sometimes he felt as though he was a burden. One day as I kneeled, putting his shoes on him, he began to cry. Dear Heart said he didn't know why I was there. He wondered how could I put aside everything in my own life just to care for him. Then he said his sons should put him in a home, and I should get back to my life.

"You are part of my life," I explained. "I am here because I chose to be. No one is holding a gun to my head." Then I told him the story of Ruth from the Bible.

As I went about my daily tasks, I thought about his pride and how he must be feeling. He couldn't even bathe himself. Being dependent on someone else was not how he wanted things to be. There had to be a way to make him think the score could be evened. I knew Steve had been known to make a few bets, so I came up with an idea that was sure to warm the cockles of his bookmaker's heart.

I announced that I had a wager for him. He could take it or leave it. He perked up. I told him the odds were likely that he would pass on before me. I could be in an accident or drop dead from a heart attack, but I bet I would outlive him.

"Here's the deal," I explained. "When I get to heaven, you meet me there with your late wife, Sarah." I had heard so many good things about Ed's mother that I really would like to meet her. "When I see you standing next to her at the pearly gates, we'll call the parlay paid in full." My thinking was right up his alley.

Steve winked and said, "You've got yourself a deal."

Several hours later, he called for me from the television room. His head was bent low and he said, "About that bet . . . I've been a rogue all my life. If there is a hell, I'm destined to go there."

I said, "Is that so? I guess you haven't heard about King David. You've probably sent dozens of men to their death, huh?"

"Well no, I never killed anybody."

"You're chances of getting to heaven are as good as King David's were."

"How could that be?"

I explained the way anyone gets to heaven is because they trust God to get them there. They believe God's son died to pay the penalty God requires for our sins, and they sincerely accept Christ as the Lord over their lives.

"David trusted God," I challenged. "You can too." Any gambling man would be foolish not to take a chance.

This is the hardest thing to understand for people like Steve and me. Most of our lives are spent with our backs to the wall. We are used to matching wits and thinking up ways to get what we want. Turning everything over to a higher power seems too easy, and we are afraid to trust.

Asking for forgiveness is never difficult. A quick review of our lives shows that we missed the mark and fell short of what God intends for us.

What happened next will live on in my soul forever. My Dear Heart asked me to help him pray. In a childlike way, he reached out and made peace with his Maker.

During the next six months, Dear Heart shared the secrets of his soul with me. He told me things he had never talked about in his life. Our bond grew as the days passed. Soon we had established our routine. At 4:00 P.M., I read the Bible. At first he wasn't interested, but he wanted to please me. It became a very uplifting time of the day for us both. Soon he became eager to hear me read. He asked questions. If I ran late with my chores, he checked his watch and coughed.

Steve told me about the church he and his family had attended and the monsignor he admired. He said if he had a last wish, it would be to see Monsignor Kantor.

At the mere mention of a Catholic church, I felt very uneasy. Old memories flooded my mind of Michael's death. I had stood by his little white casket, crying my heart out, while a Catholic priest sprinkled holy water and mumbled some words in Latin. Tears had stung my eyes so badly that I could barely see.

The priest had looked at me and said, "What are you crying for? He's better off to be out of the miseries of life."

It was two days before Christmas, and I was eighteen years old.

Somehow I managed to push aside my own feelings and think about Dear Heart and his wish. I sat at his kitchen table, wrote an emotionally charged letter, and addressed it in care of Sacred Heart Church. I explained who I was and stated that my concern was for the last wish of an old man who wanted more than anything else to see Monsignor Kantor.

I didn't know if my letter would reach the monsignor or if he was even alive, but I prayed that he was and that he would at least write to Dear Heart.

Weeks passed. I had forgotten about the letter when a big, black limousine drove up in the driveway. I didn't even have time to change my clothes or clear the breakfast dishes. The first man to step out was the deacon who usually came to give Dear Heart communion. Following the deacon was none other than the monsignor himself. No one had to tell me who he was. And there I stood in my pink flannel pajamas.

We exchanged greetings. The monsignor asked where Steve was. I directed him to the room upstairs and watched him throw up his arms and say, "Where is my Steven?" Dear Heart stared at him as if he were gazing at Jesus Christ in the flesh. I was taken aback at seeing Dear Heart's dream come true for him. It was a touching scene that I will never forget.

I changed my clothes and went to the kitchen to finish cleaning.

To my surprise, the monsignor came searching for me. He took my hand and asked, "When was your last confession, my child?"

"Last night," I replied.

He said, "There were no churches open for confession last night."

A defiant me stated that there was in my room, while I was on my knees in prayer.

"That's good enough for me," he said. "I want you to be a part of our communion and healing service."

I was stunned. He didn't wait for a response but lead me upstairs where the deacon and Dear Heart were waiting.

We were instructed to form a circle and hold hands. The monsignor prayed and then gave us communion. He anointed our foreheads with oil in the sign of the cross and called upon the Holy Spirit for healing. I held tight to Dear Heart's hand and didn't know what to expect. We stood there with our eyes closed and our heads bowed, and I wondered if they could hear my knees knocking.

The roof didn't open up. There was no thunder or lightning. No one shook or fell over like they did on television. Yet, there was no doubt that He came. There was a joyous feeling in the room and comfort beyond any earthly experience as He encircled us in the warmth and power of His love. At the close of the service, the monsignor blessed us and began to sing "How Great Thou Art" in a tone so pure and sweet that it reached into the depths of my soul. When he started to sing "I'll Never Forget You, My Friend" to Dear Heart I had to excuse myself.

In the privacy of my room, the anguish that I had carried around inside of me for so long left with the tears that flowed from my eyes. At last I understood that it wasn't the fault of the Catholic Church that had brought me such intense pain. One insensitive priest had said a hurtful thing to a grieving mother, and his words left a deep wound that had refused to heal.

Dear Heart passed away soon after our visit from the monsignor. Nevertheless, there was a healing in the upstairs room that day—a healing of the heart, my heart. There were no cameras to record the event. Nothing was written in the newspaper. No one was paid for the service. Monsignor Kantor came because he cared and was lead by the Holy Spirit to a dying old man and a broken-hearted woman whom God had not forgotten.

I will see Dear Heart again some day when I get to heaven. He'll be standing beside an angel named Sarah. He will say that he is making good on our arrangement and tell me not to forget to mark the contract accordingly.

I'll be happy to see him—even though I know he'll ask what took me so long! He'll say, "It's about time you got here."

Then he will tell me he has been standing in that same spot for years, honoring his part of our little agreement. He'll say it again, just in case I have developed a hearing problem. He'll have that sly smile on his face. He'll hug me and tell me he has missed me.

He'll say, "Billie, dear, it is with great pleasure that I introduce you to my wife, my angel, Sarah."

She'll welcome me to heaven. She'll have a twinkle in her eyes like the one she gave to her sons. I'll tell her how sweet it is to finally meet her.

Dear Heart will be looking better than Cary Grant. His limp will be gone. He'll say that he has loved me forever in spite of the fact that I was Irish. Then he'll say that it really was a shame that I wasn't Ukrainian or Polish.

And then I'll say, "Glory be, Dear Heart, darlin', is that yourself I'm lookin' at? Top o' the mornin' to ya. Been waitin' long? Isn't it grand to be seein' each other in a place sprinkled with stardust? 'Tis so lovely and green. Why, if I hadn't seen the pearly gates, I'd swear 'twas a little bit of the Emerald Isle we were standin' in and not heaven itself. It is so good to be home, sure and begorra, I have missed you too."

CHAPTER 33

· · · · · · · · · · · · · · ·

A Sweet, Sweet Spirit

fter Dear Heart passed away, I didn't know what to do with myself. Ed was busy building our dream home and couldn't handle me even on a good day. The attic was too hot, and I felt uncomfortable in my own home with three strangers. I took a job as a live-in caregiver to a stroke victim. Her name was Mildred Bugge, and she was an unforgettable old dear. I fell in love with her the first time I saw her.

At Mildred's door, I was greeted by a girl named Jenny who was in charge of Mildred's care at the time. Mildred was sitting across the room in a reclining chair. Jenny conducted the interview. Mildred could not speak or walk. She did have the use of one side of her body. And she spoke with the most incredible eyes I have ever seen. She made aaaaahhhh sounds for "yes" and oooooo sounds for "no."

When the interview was over, I walked to Mildred, held her hand, and looked into those eyes of hers. I saw some part of me in there that was strangely familiar. Jenny told me that as soon as I walked out the door, Mildred started hollering and pointing to the door and to herself. She wanted me. I moved in two days later.

The year that I spent with my Mildred in her cottage by the Chesapeake Bay was the happiest year of my life—mostly because I felt free to be. There was a sweet, sweet spirit in that place.

Mildred was a big-boned Norwegian girl. It wasn't easy to change her diaper, get her dressed, and move her around, but I didn't care what I had to do. I did it without thinking. I was happy to be there.

Mildred's stepson Norman and his wife Nancy were wonderful to me. Anything I needed, they supplied. They opened a checking account and put my name on it. They couldn't always drive from Ashland, Virginia, over two hours away. They were getting on in years themselves.

I shopped for the best of everything and had something good cooking all the time. Mildred loved to eat. I opened the windows, turned on the music, and danced. Every single day of that year, someone called, sent a card, or dropped by for a visit. At first I thought they were just checking me out, but that was not the case at all. Mildred was loved. On Mildred's birthday, she received over fifty cards! Of course, I had to read every one of them to her, some twice.

Dennis Burgess was Mildred's boyfriend. They had once lived in the same neighborhood with their spouses who had long since passed away. They had a wonderful friendship. Old "D. B." came by the house every morning. He was eighty-five and playing golf nearly every day. He called me "Baby Doll." Before he left for the day, he'd hug and thank me for taking good care of Mildred.

The Reverend Kenneth Carbaugh was Mildred's pastor. He is one of the few truly holy men to ever cross my path. He visited because he genuinely cared.

He told me about Our Savior Lutheran Church just down the road. Mildred had worked tirelessly for the church for thirty-five years. She spent so much time there, some folks thought she was the assistant pastor. Mildred was in charge of everything. She was the one to call if you needed a helping hand. It was Mildred who went to college with young girls and got them settled in when their mothers couldn't make it. It was Mildred who was mistress of ceremony when daughters of the church were married. Mildred loved them all.

Pastor Ken was newly married to a fiery, red-haired woman, Trisha. There was something about her that was interesting and good. He was a widower when they had married. His late wife, Elizabeth, and Mildred had been close friends. Trisha helped my understanding of the church and Mildred's role there. In order to get to know all the people involved in Mildred's life, I gathered her photo albums and went through years of memories, while she sat beside me in her chair. She gave me the aaaaahhhh for her good friends. A long aaaaaaaaaaaaaaahhhhhhhh was a great friend.

The photos revealed Mildred as a fun-loving old girl. One picture showed her jumping up and down on a hotel bed with another lady. Another revealed her leg. Others showed rows of tables and Mildred putting out enough food to feed an army.

Ed adored Mildred. When he visited, Mildred grinned like a cat. She really thought he was hot stuff. He was the only one strong enough to take her to the beach directly down the street from her house. She loved and longed for the waters of her beautiful Chesapeake Bay. Ed ran while pushing Mildred in her wheelchair. They raced up and down the streets of her beloved neighborhood. Mildred felt the wind in her hair and on her face, and she was happy.

Ed was moving right along on the house and doing a great job. I had six hours off each day, and while I was out, I picked up wallpaper samples and tile and things to select for the house. Mildred was a grand help. I held up the samples, and she smiled or frowned. We looked through magazines and decorating books by the armful.

About four months after I had moved into the house, Norman told me Mildred was running out of cash. He was considering putting his mother in a nursing home, and he was agonizing about what it might do to her. Norman was seventy and his darling wife was almost blind. I cried all night and thought how empty my life would be without Mildred. I told Norman that I would work and keep track of my hours. He could pay me when Mildred passed away and her house sold. A lawyer drew up some papers in case something were to happen to Norman. I thanked God for my brilliant idea.

One day while I was talking to Pastor Ken, the phone rang. It was my son Eddy, whom I hadn't heard from in ages. He said that he wanted to talk to me, that he had something important to say. I gave him directions, and soon he was standing in the kitchen. He had a young girl with him who stayed in the background.

Eddy stood close to me and spoke from his heart. He told me he was so sorry for causing me such pain, for every unkind word and deed. Would I forgive him and be his mother again? He said he loved me and wanted me to be a part of his life.

Would I? Dear Sweet Jesus, how I had prayed for this precious moment.

Eddy was in Virginia Beach because he had a court date. He was lucky they hadn't put him in jail for running away from traffic violations and other petty offenses. The girl standing by the door was an angel, and Eddy was in love. Kathie Childress would not consent to marriage to my son until she saw Eddy reconciled with his mother. She had insisted that she see it with her own eyes. Eddy promised to pay me back every cent of the money he had borrowed, which he did.

My sweet, freckle-faced "strawberry," "Eddy Spaghetti," was a man. He had learned to combine that joyous fun-loving nature that was part of his father with the tenacity he had inherited from his mother. It was a winning combination. Love brought it all together in the arms of his angel, Kathie.

After they left, I crawled in bed with my Mildred and cried like a baby. She cuddled me close and stroked my hair with her good hand. Her aaaaahhhh was comfort for my soul.

Mildred knew everything about me. I was blessed to find someone who would listen to every detail of my life without them telling me to go fly a kite. When my sister Alice met Mildred, she cried as she saw the compassion in the old dear's eyes. My sister sensed what was in Mildred's soul and understood why I considered Mildred my confidante and my friend.

One day while I was out running errands, a nurse dropped Mildred while she was in her lift. Mildred had hit her head. Pastor Ken met me at the hospital. We both knew our Mildred was slipping away. He placed his hands on her head and prayed, "Heavenly Father, welcome your child Mildred into your kingdom, and in the name of Jesus, we ask that you forgive her sins and grant her life everlasting. Amen."

Mildred was in a coma for two weeks. Nancy called and asked me to talk with Mildred and give her permission to die. She said that sometimes unselfish people like Mildred find it difficult to leave the ones they love, thinking that they are still needed.

I sat beside her hospital bed and marveled at how beautiful her skin was; it had taken on a translucent appearance. I knew she was very close to God. With her hand in mine, I thanked her for every day of our year and for the happiness she gave me. I told her how selfish I was to want to keep her here when I knew that she had places to go and things to do. For some reason, I was able to speak freely without choking on my words.

When I kissed her face and said, "Go in peace, dear friend," I knew she would be leaving very soon. Besides hospital staff, I was the last person to see Mildred alive.

Mildred was buried on Memorial Day. Her late husband, Ragnor, had died on the same day in May, many years ago. I moped around for a long time. Norman told me at the funeral that at the moment his mother died, he felt her spirit in his room.

Nancy said, "He sat right up in the bed, felt a chill, and made the remark that maybe he was coming down with a cold."

Then the phone rang and he knew that his mother had come to say farewell.

Maybe it was selfish, but I wondered why she didn't come to see me.

The night before my birthday, I had a dream about Mildred. It was approximately two weeks since she had passed away. She was lying still in her bed and then she sat up and began talking to me. The dream woke me and I heard her say, "Happy Birthday," and I felt her hug my entire body. I sat there laughing. I knew she had waited to send me good wishes on my birthday. No one will ever convince me that it was only a dream.

To this day it is difficult to watch *Wheel of Fortune* without crying and thinking of those wondrous days with Mildred. Every evening, I pushed Mildred's wheelchair close to the television and sat beside her. We played the game together. I'd guess and she'd cheer. Mildred would take my hand in hers and kiss my fingers.

The first time she did that, I glanced over at her and said, "You love me, don't you, Mildred?"

She placed our hands above her heart and said, "Aaaaaaaahhhhhhhh."

I will see her again someday. She'll be waiting just across the beautiful water on some distant shore and grinning like a big cat.

The tenants moved out of my house and I felt more comfortable there. Ed and I were getting tired of living out of boxes. I spent a lot of time at the new house, sweeping and loading debris into our truck. I can't count the loads of trash we hauled to the dump. We lost weight and we aggravated each other like children.

Eddy and Kathie were married in Greenville, South Carolina, on July 18, 1992. My darling granddaughter, Elizabeth, and I drove down for the wedding. Kathie has a warm and loving family. I was so proud and happy for my son. My new daughter-in-law had attended Greenville Technical College for two years. She had a good job at the Greenville News-Piedmont Company. She was more than an answer to my prayers. I was floating on a cloud. And, yes, she did want children!

Sara Elizabeth Tolson was born a year later. Two years later, my grandson, Wesley Aaron, was born. Today, Kathie is a full-time mommy. Eddy has his own home-repair business. Is God good or what?

In April 1993 we moved into our home, which had one working bathroom and no carpeting. The house had taken Ed three years to build—three long years. I do not recommend building a home the way we built ours. We ran out of money twice because our houses were not selling. By the time we ironed everything out, we were exhausted and close to divorce.

Our home is so incredible I have to pinch myself sometimes to make sure I am not dreaming. The house is an English Tudor built with warm brick and stone. It has six tons of Tennessee Bluestone around the front entrance and in the massive fireplace. The stone in the fireplace is twenty feet high and measures ten feet wide. I named this place Bluestone Manor. We have a bronze plaque with the name and year of occupancy written in large script letters on one of the brick stanchions at the edge of the driveway.

Builders from all over our area came to marvel at the house that Ed built. No one can believe how it all came together. People ask me where I went to school to learn design and interior decorating. My advisor in decorating was Lynnette Jennings. I faithfully watched her television program and wrote down everything. When I was stumped with a seemingly unsolvable problem, she advised hiring a professional by the hour. I'd hired someone for one hour—that's all the help I needed. I still like to do some things on my own.

For the important matters of life, though, I've learned—often the hard way—not to rely solely on myself. "I can do all things through Christ which strengtheneth me" (Phil. 4:13).

Section IV.
Where Are
They Now?

CHAPTER 34

My Sister,
My Friend

Diane and Chuck were married after they both finished college and moved to Charlottesville, Virginia. They had a baby every year for four years—Sharon, Steven, Susan, and Sean. They bought a large tract of land with a view of the Blue Ridge Mountains and made a family project of clearing the lot for their dream home. Chuck retired from his job as a Highway Research Scientist with the state of Virginia. He then went into business as a consultant. Diane is a retired nurse practitioner.

Several years ago, Diane and Chuck visited us at our summer home. I couldn't believe Diane's statement that she was seeing a psychiatrist for depression. Where had I been? Why hadn't I seen that I wasn't the only one who had pain? She admitted she sometimes envied me for being able to laugh, even when things were falling apart. I had spent my entire life feeling inadequate, while my dear sister had frustrations that ran deeper than I could imagine. She had fears and insecurities not unlike my own. Maybe we weren't so different after all.

As I listened, I saw that my role in our childhood as a failure had afforded me some escape from the pressure of being perfect. When I had fallen on my face, which was often, the adults in my life just shrugged their shoulders and said, "Oh well, that's Billie."

There was no freedom for Diane. She had to be a parent to her own parents and siblings, a model student, and a perfect mother. After she left home, she was thin, anemic, and fearful that she might have to drop out of college to return home and care for her family. She felt guilty at mealtimes because she knew we were hungry at home. It was a miracle that she graduated second in her class.

It's no wonder everyone thought Diane was a saint. Rather, she was a girl who had been robbed of her precious childhood. She attempted to hold up her whole world, while standing on the pedestal others had made for her. When she needed help, rather than burden anyone, she pushed until her strength was gone and she could no longer be the picture of perfection that we had painted her. I think our family put her on that pedestal because we all desperately needed someone to look up to.

Today, Diane is more beautiful than ever and at peace with the past. She and Chuck built their Cape Cod dream house and now live in Crozet, Virginia. Chuck and Diane belong to a hiking club. They have friends from all over the world. Her house smells like freshly baked bread and feels like home in every room. Diane's children grew up secure in the knowledge that they are loved and wanted. She is a proud, picture-carrying, bragging grandmother of eight: Lisa, Rachel, Hannah, Mary Eileen, Patrick, Haley, Chuck, and Jake.

The shrine I have for my sister is in my heart. In place of flowers and candles, I have memories. I have fond remembrances of a girl who bought Goobers with her hard-to-come-by lunch money and shared them with me and a dog that had followed us to the bus stop, a girl filled with love for her family, who never asked anything in return.

Our Father in heaven sent one of His dearest angels to be my very own sister because He knew my world would get harsh now and then. She walked beside me and held my trembling hand when we were children, she called me friend when we came of age, and God saw that it was good. It was very good.

CHAPTER 35

It Is No Secret

All through the years, I had called to check on Grandmama. But two years before she passed away, I had an overwhelming urge to see her. I found her sitting in a torn-up chair, wearing a ragged, stained dress. Her hair, which once hung in curls tied back with pretty bows, was gray, matted, and stringy. Her once clean house was a mess. Garbage, including bags of rotten potatoes crawling with maggots, was piled up in the kitchen. I wondered how things could have gotten that bad. Where were her children? I felt so ashamed. Where had I been?

Early the next morning I went back to her house with my cleaning supplies. The first thing on my schedule was to give my grandmother a bath and shampoo her hair. The thought of being seen naked by her granddaughter made her very uneasy. I put a seat in the tub for Grandmama to sit on while I soaped her body. To ease her tension, I sang Grandmama's song that had comforted me many years before:

It is no secret what God can do.
What He's done for others, He'll do for you. . . .[1]

As I sang, her squeaky old voice chimed in—she remembered every word. We sang and sang. Then we laughed and cried and held each other. We did that every week for eight months.

At the end of my visits, we sipped coffee and talked. I had heard many stories about my grandparents, mostly from my parents, but it never mattered to me whether they were true or not. Grandmama and Granddaddy loved me and they were good to me. Grandmama knew that I didn't care about the stories, but now she wanted me to know the truth. Over those eight months, she told me the story of her life—an incredible story of love, betrayal, and courage.

Grandmama was only fourteen when she married Granddaddy. She had left home to get away from her own father. He had molested her sister, and she was afraid that he might do the same thing to her. Her first child was born when she was fifteen. She dearly loved Granddaddy, and they had eight wonderful years together. But her love died and her heart was broken when he had an affair with a red-haired woman. By this time she had four children. She could not drive and had no place to go. They agreed to stay together and raise their family.

Periodically over that long life together, Grandmama had turned to a particular man for the comfort she thought she needed to carry on. Thankfully, before Granddaddy died, she and Granddaddy made peace with each other and the Lord. Still, some of their children never really got over it all.

One day while we were sitting at her table, Grandmama got misty-eyed. "Biddy," she said, "I have something special I've been saving, and I want you to have it. It's all I have of my mother. I have always treasured it."

She directed me to an old cabinet. Hidden at the bottom, wrapped in rags, was a small cut glass vase. When I pulled it out, her face lit up and she said, "Take it Biddy; it's yours." It was difficult for me to speak, but I looked deep into her eyes and thanked her, telling her that I was so honored to receive her most prized possession. On the way back to my home that afternoon, my hand stroked the little vase lying beside me on the car seat. I couldn't contain my tears. I realized it was the best she had, and she had chosen to give it to me.

Aunt Ruthie drove to Virginia Beach for Grandmama's ninetieth birth-day. I asked the bakers to decorate the cake with Grandmama's favorite pink roses. I picked up my mother and drove to Norfolk. By this time, Grandmama was bedridden and needed full time care. Her caregiver, Kim, was a nice girl. I could tell that she was good to my grandmother. The house was clean, and my grandmother was clean and contented enough under the circumstances.

Before we celebrated, I watched Aunt Ruthie lovingly spoon-feed Grandmama the cream of broccoli soup she had made especially for her. Grandmama was so happy to see her cake, even though she was too weak to blow out the candles. Something in all of us told us this would be our last celebration together.

Mama's younger brother moved his girlfriend into Grandmama's house after that party. Jimmy said he would take care of everything. I took Mama to visit her mother several times, and we saw that she was doing as well as could be expected. The light in her eyes, though, was growing dim.

Aunt Ruthie came from Florida as often as she could to see her mother. We all noticed her fading away. My father came down from the mountains, and he and I went for a visit. Daddy could hardly speak, as he was so sad to see the once vibrant woman he had called mother-in-law for thirty years. There were genuine, tender feelings between them. They held each other for a moment. Then Grandmama told Daddy she loved him and was happy to see him. Daddy said he loved her too. They wished each other blessings from God. Later, Daddy and I drove away in tears.

I saw Grandmama in a nearby hospital the day before she died. She was alone in a room in the intensive care unit. The nurses informed me that she was in a coma and wouldn't hear me or respond to me. I didn't believe it. I took her small frail hand in mine and bent close to her face.

"It's me Grandmama. It's Biddy." Her right foot moved.

I told her how much she meant to me and how I would miss her, but I knew it was time for her to go. Again, her foot moved. My throat ached.

I didn't think I'd be able to speak further, but the strength came. "Don't be afraid, old friend. You're going to go somewhere special, a place where no one will ever hurt you or break your heart again. The angels will come for you, and when you see the light, walk right into it, and soon you'll see the face of God."

Tears rolled off my face onto Grandmama's cheeks. "Good-bye. I love you," I said, and I kissed her face for the last time. Then in that room, with just the two of us and the angels, I sang the last few words of her song, our song: "With arms wide open He'll pardon you. It is no secret what God can do. . . ."

Grandmama was laid to rest next to Granddaddy on a cold and rainy day. Jimmy was in charge of the arrangements, which were a mess. At ninety-one years old, she had been a mother, a great-grandmother, and a great-great-grandmother. She had outlived her firstborn. Only three of her five remaining children were present at her memorial service. Jimmy was not one of them. A distant relative from out of town gave her eulogy. No one put an obituary in the newspaper because everyone assumed it had been done. There was nothing written to say that she had even lived before she died. The pauper's casket that held her body was not nearly good enough for her remains inside.

I wanted to scream, "She was so much more than this!"

How could I measure the worth of the memories she had left in my heart? There was no way to really tell the world what a grandmother had done for a lost little girl. Only I would remember the days in the swing, the nights on the couch, the praise for a song, the encouragement to reach for the stars. Who would ever again call me "Biddy" and see the wounded child in me, that frizzy-haired moppet who was always searching for love?

But Aunt Ruthie was there. She kissed me and tried to make it better. She couldn't make it stop hurting. She was hurting too. I saw my grandmother in Aunt Ruthie's eyes.

I'll see Grandmama again when I get to heaven. She'll be the one sitting in the porch swing, with her arms outstretched. Her dark curls will be pulled back with pretty ribbons and bows from her full face. Her dress will be brightly colored. There will be a jeweled pin on her collar. And she'll be singing. . . .

. . . .

CHAPTER 36

You Are My Sunshine

Elizabeth Noel Elliott is twenty years old now! In June 1998, she graduated with honors from Halifax County High-school in "Cornfield County" and attended Danville Community College. My granddaughter was active in the drama club and had leading roles in school productions.

And, yes, we did sing and laugh and play. Her favorite memory is of a tea party at our cabin on the lake. We got all "dolled up": long dresses, makeup—the works. Our serving set was a lovely china teapot and delicate cups. The napkins were two old socks, which we used to daintily dab the corners of our mouths. We held our pinkies up in ladylike fashion. Her name was always Margaret; mine was Mabel. We affected British accents and talked about Prince Charles and his rather large ears, deciding that we were, no doubt, distant cousins.

Oh, how I loved to take her outside and wrap my arms around her like Grandmama had done with me. We had the moon, stars, and each other. She liked to put her head in my lap while I told her stories and traced around her little eyes with my fingertips. When she cried for her mother, I was so thankful to be there to ease the pain. She looked forward to those nights out on the deck, and I lived for each moment. She didn't care that I sounded like Edith Bunker, she loved to hear me sing "My little girl, pink and white, as peaches and cream is she. . . ."

We had so many songs and so many nights together in the summer and in the winter when the ground was covered with snow. We chose "You Are My Sunshine" as our song.

Being a grandmother is my finest hour. I am wiser and more patient. I learned from years of practice making mistakes with my own children. It's a wonder they will speak to me. They wouldn't buy my story about my middle-child syndrome, but they are forgiving souls. Besides, they can't get rid of me. I keep showing up at weddings and parties. They can't deny me. The family resemblance is too strong.

Elizabeth has heard about some of my failures. They don't apply to her, just as the tales about my own grandmother hadn't mattered to me. Thank God, all she remembers is love, sweet love.

We had a big celebration when Elizabeth turned eighteen. The house was filled with relatives and friends. I gave her the diamond solitaire necklace that I had promised her when she was a little girl.

My granddaughter filled a great void inside me. She gave me the opportunity to give something back. I pray that she will reach for the stars and be good to herself. If she can dream big dreams and believe that every good thing is hers already, she'll find her pot of gold. My darling girl has everything right inside of herself. I'll hound her if she forgets for one moment that she is special and loved.

CHAPTER 37

. . . .

'Tis You, 'Tis You

My silver-haired daddy is hanging in there at eighty-six. He lives in Ridgeley, West Virginia. My father is the sole surviving member of his family. He has shared his life with a very nice lady, Pauline, for over twenty years. He had open-heart surgery in 1997 on his birthday. He's in great shape for the shape he's in.

Everyone was worried about him after the operation. He looked so small and frail with tubes in his nose and throat. He weighed less than 120 pounds. Machines attached to his body monitored numerous bodily functions. Seeing him helpless caused me to think about so many things. He has made an earnest effort to make amends for his shortcomings as a father. He is loved. There is peace in the hearts of his children. Daddy is coming around the last bend in the road of his life. Who am I to cast a stone?

Daddy has spent a great deal of time planning his funeral. He was a chief storekeeper in the United States Navy. He wants to be buried in his chief's uniform. He asked me, if I could, to get the clothing and hat for him at the Navy Exchange, which I did. Diane is in charge of the music he wants played at the service. A funeral is a once-in-a-lifetime thing, not to be taken lightly.

Daddy's idea of heaven is that dear land across the Irish Sea. My father will never really get rid of me altogether. I'll join him in the hereafter, and he will have forgotten what a pain I was. He'll be the one with the smiling Irish eyes. I will sing his song, Danny boy, "Tis you, tis you, must go and I must bide."

Daddy will be very happy when he gets to heaven, and tall, too. When I stroll through the gates, I bet he'll be standing next to my brother Larry. I'll recognize Larry; he'll be the baby with jug ears just like mine.

The poor man had a tremendous handicap: me. There was never a shred of doubt that I was a thorn in his side. Who knew he would sire his own pint-sized sparring partner? He did the best he could with what he had to work with, which is what we all do. He'll get a gold star for his fatherly effort with me.

By then, Grandma Hughes will probably have all the ladies organized into an astral auxiliary. She won't be hard to find. She'll be the one wearing big celestial earrings, and her room will be full of heavenly greeting cards picturing real angels.

My grandfather will no doubt be wearing his game warden hat. He might be playing minor league baseball, as he did when he was young.

Uncle Owen will be smiling really big and wearing a conductor's hat for sure. He might even have his own train and take me all over heaven to show me off. I'll be glad to see him. I'll tell him he would have made a great father.

Aunt Evelyn will be romping in the clouds with a basset hound named Jasper. Her face won't be wrinkled up anymore form sucking on all of those lemons.

Aunt Genevieve will no doubt be watching reruns of winning Notre Dame games on the biggest screen you ever saw. She won't be too busy to stop and give me a hug or maybe make me a sandwich.

Uncle Les will still have his freckles. He'll probably jump out from behind a cloud and say "boo!" a zillion times. But he won't scare me. He never did.

CHAPTER 38

Alice Blue Gown

Mama lives alone in the house that her late husband built. She suffered a stroke and has problems with motor skills, resulting from complications of hydrocephalus. Even with all that, she manages to stay in the home she loves. Most of her friends are gone now. Her partner in crime, Aunt Edna, died. She's probably in heaven still singing "I love him so because he's just my Bill," just like she did on earth, when she entertained us with her wonderful voice.

Mama would like to find a man. She has been known to place advertisements in the senior section of the newspaper. You know the kind: "Saucy lady seeks mature gentleman for quiet evenings and possible romance." I have gone with her on occasion to scope out potential suitors. It took one old fellow so long to get out of the car, that I was getting worried. By the time he got into the restaurant for lunch, it was almost dinnertime. We could barely finish our lunch. He had to hurry home because he said it was getting dark outside.

My mother says there is plenty of fire in her furnace. However, most men her age can only remember their names and social security numbers. There have been several nice men in her life since Peck died. However, the romances broke up, mostly because of the night blindness thing. Mama would like to be able to go places.

Like my grandmother, Mama was only fourteen when she married. My father claimed he didn't know she was a juvenile when they met. Mama said he did know, and Aunt Nona backs her up. Whatever the case, she should have been home playing with paper dolls. Instead, she was in a dance hall looking for a train out. She says that she loved Daddy when they began their life together. At least it seemed like love to her, but she was just a child. What did she know about being a wife at fourteen or a mother at sixteen? She never had the chance to be a girl, and before she knew it, she had a house full of children. Mama couldn't figure out how to grow up and be a mother at the same time. She did the best she knew how to do.

Mama will probably outlive us all. If it so happens that I go first, I'll see her coming. She'll be all dressed up and happy at last. My mother will know for sure that she was loved. Granddaddy and Grandmama will be waiting. They'll be playing her tune through the grand celestial woofers in the sky. Aunt Edna will be singing:

In your sweet little Alice blue gown
When you first wandered down into town[1]

It is impossible for me to think about my mother without thinking about her second husband. When he was a little boy, his Aunt Minnie often referred to him as "Peck's Bad Boy" because of his mischievous, happy nature. She got the idea from some of the characters of famed author George Wilbur Peck. His lovable, mirth-provoking "Peck's Bad Boy" sketches thrilled and delighted readers throughout the country in the early 1900s.

Peck Hunter was a rare and precious jewel. Before he passed away from cancer, I had an opportunity to do something for him. He spent most of the time resting to conserve what little strength he had left. One day while I was dusting under his bed, I felt his hand tousle my hair. I looked up and saw his smiling face. He said, "I've always wanted to do that." He was grinning like a possum when he said it.

I had a golden opportunity to tell him that I loved him for his goodness. If I could have, I would have taken some of his pain. He told me all about how he built his home by himself and how proud he was of the work he had done. Even though I had heard it before, I didn't mind at all. It was a lovely story. I wish he could tell me every detail one more time so I could see his eyes light up.

While he was in the hospital, I stayed with him almost every night until his daughter Linda arrived. She was there every night from midnight until around eight o'clock in the morning, at which time she went home to tend to her two young children.

I wouldn't trade those moments spent with him, because it gave me a chance to say thank you. Peck couldn't speak, he was unconscious, and we all knew it was just a matter of time before God would take him home.

I held his hand and told him that my sisters, brother, and I were grateful that he had come along and had taken good care of Mama. I don't know what we would have done without him. I don't know what she would have done if he hadn't provided for her. He left enough to take care of her for the rest of her life.

I believe he heard me.

Jonathan "Peck" Hunter was a southern gentleman. He departed this life on April 15, 1987.

I'll see him again when I get to heaven. He'll be grinning like the mischievous "Peck's Bad Boy" of long ago. He'll be holding a clapping toy monkey like the one he loved to carry in the Shriner's Parade. He'll be the one wearing the fez.

CHAPTER 39

My Brother, the Hero

My only brother, Joseph Arthur Hughes, is a hero! I remember when his claim to fame was twirling a cap gun around his finger. Now he has a real gun and a badge. As a child, his dream was to be a police officer. When he was old enough to pursue that dream, he did not meet the height requirements. Instead, Joe joined the navy, got out, then went back to school. He graduated from a high school in Fort Ashby, West Virginia, and continued on to college. He retired from civil service prior to joining the Portsmouth Police Department.

Later, the height requirements for the police force changed, and Joe finally fulfilled his lifetime ambition. He was Rookie of the Year at fifty years old! Joe was written up in the local newspaper for saving the life of Grover D. Madlock, a resident of Portsmouth, Virginia.

My brother and his beautiful wife, Robin, raised two sons, Brent and Brett, who are on their own and doing well. Joe and Robin live in Chesapeake, Virginia. Their home should be featured in a magazine. Robin does wonderful things with silk flowers. She still turns heads and refuses to get old. She hasn't gained an ounce in years. I bet she has never had to keep three sizes of clothes in her closet.

Joe and his wife have a granddaughter who is the light of their lives. Little Brianna looks like her grandmother. Joe's two sons from his first marriage are grown men. Oscar lives in Maine, and Joe Jr. lives with his wife and son, Benjamin, in Italy, where I "ran into" him a few years ago on a trip with Ed! I'm still basking in the glow of that reunion.

CHAPTER 40

Partners in Crime

My hooky-playing, pie-snatching, former partner in crime is over fifty years old! I don't know what happened to all the years. It seems like just yesterday we stood at the bus stop on Chesapeake street and I flipped a coin to determine our day's schedule. Of course, no matter what the coin showed, our plan always turned out to be the movies and not school. We shared some great times.

Kathleen had legs like a movie star. She could have been a professional dancer. Even though Kathleen was the "runt of the litter," she didn't get short changed where it really matters. She's got a heart as big as a sturdy oak tree. When I think about her, I see her twirling around in a dress with a hoop skirt. The hearth in our living room on Lesner Avenue was her stage, and she liked to put on shows for us.

Her girlfriend, Martha, took lessons, and Kathleen picked right up on tap dancing routines. She had one long curl hanging down the middle of her back until I gave her a haircut, which she really didn't want. My barbering career started early.

My sister and her husband Rick lived in Wisconsin for twenty years. He recently retired from the police department. She was an office manager in charge of everything from files to payroll at a car body shop.

They recently moved to New Bern, North Carolina. Kathleen had enough of snow and ice.

Their sons, Kevin and Rick, are grown men. Rick Jr. and his wife, Marcia, have two children: Steven and Caylin. Kevin and his wife Leann have a daughter, Kevalee.

Kathleen and Rick enjoy playing golf and traveling. One of their favorite vacation spots is Jamaica, Mon. Considering they lived in Wisconsin so long, it isn't difficult to figure out why they find beaches so appealing.

. . . .

CHAPTER 41

Little Baby
Sister of Mine

My youngest sister Alice isn't Alice anymore, but she is as beautiful as ever. She has changed her name to Alexis. She wanted her own name.

When I think of her, I often see an old McDonald's commercial with a boy, his sister, and french fries. Later as an adult, the boy sees his grown sister in their favorite McDonald's, and he remembers a tender moment.

Alexis has a generous heart, and I know that she's on her way to a good place in this world. She and her husband John are very successful in the business community. They have their own consulting firm in Chesapeake, Virginia. Not long ago they were written up in the local newspaper and chosen small business of the year. John invented some very snazzy computer equipment and was smart enough to patent all his ideas. They live in Virginia Beach on the waterfront.

It is difficult to believe that even Alexis is over forty and a grandmother. Her children—Kimberly, Toby, Joshua, and Johnnie—are not babies anymore. Kim has two children now: Bryan Patrick and his little brother Kyle Owen.

I've always heard that when the baby of the family starts going gray, the rest of the clan is really getting old. Sometimes that is pretty scary, but other times it isn't so bad . . . I'll still never be the oldest.

. . . .

CHAPTER 42

The Best for Last

U ncle Bill passed away in 1986. It took Aunt Nona awhile to get her bearings and adjust to being single. She had been married most of her life. She lives in an apartment not far from my mother. Through the years, I have kept in touch with her. She always has a smile and a great big hug for me.

I called my aunt recently for an update on her life. She summed it all up in one word: *boring!* That's light years from the truth, which I finally squeezed out of her.

Aunt Nona found a male companion in the personal section of a local magazine. She responded to an ad and met Paul Humphries. They arranged to meet at the same restaurant that Mama patronizes. One fine day, Aunt Nona found a jewel in Shoney's.

Aunt Nona isn't in the best of health. However, her apartment is full of life when her eighty-one-year-old Paul visits. They sing and dance in her living room. Besides his civil service career, Paul was a singer with a local country music band. They travel some too. Paul took Aunt Nona to Disneyland for the first time.

My Aunt Nona has a sparkle in her eyes that should have been there years ago. But she isn't complaining about lost years or what might have been. She's here and it's today. Paul's here and she's happy.

CHAPTER 43

Sitting on a Gold Mine

Uncle Johnny is still the same lovable "Huggy Bear" he's always been. If you stop by to see him, he will try to give you everything he can think of that you might want. If there is something he may have forgotten, his benevolent wife, Aunt Donna, will find it and put it in a bag for you.

You could say that my uncle had it all together, except for one thing. He is sitting on a gold mine and doesn't even know it. Somewhere in his garage sale travels, he picked up a truly gifted dog for ten bucks. I know that people will brag about their pets, maybe even stretch the truth, but an impartial third party, the Reverend Will Kiser-Lowrence of Bayside Presbyterian Church will also testify to an amazing truth about this dog.

The dog can speak in clear words when begging for goodies. He says, "I want one." This dog is not a hog—one is plenty. Not only does this incredible pooch talk, but also he removes socks from humans. What can I say? He has a sock thing. He isn't perfect. If that doesn't leave you breathless, then consider this: In an instant, that dog will flip right over on his back when hearing the word "fleas." He lies perfectly still and invites your inspection, if you are so inclined.

Despite his talents, I personally think the dog is unhappy with his appearance. He has a painfully noticeable underbite. There is no denying it to the dog—he can look in the mirror. You just can't lie to a good dog like Spike.

CHAPTER 44

My Darlingest Aunt Ruthie

My darlingest Aunt Ruthie lives in West Palm Beach, Florida, with her husband, lifetime friend, and lover, Uncle Lloyd. Through the years, Aunt Ruthie has laughed and cried with me. She relived my every step as I sent her chapter after chapter of my story and invited her critique. She sang right along with Loretta and me. She even felt my distress as I traveled Virginia Beach Boulevard in search of a job and a way out.

Last Christmas, I could not get the song "May the Good Lord Bless and Keep You" out of my mind. I called to ask my aunt if the words held any significance for her in association with her mother, my Grandmama. Aunt Ruthie said she sang that song with Grandmama all the time.

Thank you, Aunt Ruthie, for your encouragement and sweet love. You taught me how to laugh in the rain, and I love you. "May the good Lord bless and keep you till we meet again."

Aunt Ruthie and Uncle Lloyd are shining beacons of light for me and everyone who knows them. They are Divine Love in action.

....

CHAPTER 45

Jimmy

Mama's younger brother, Jimmy, died in his sleep in 1998. He was fifty-four years old and weighed over four hundred pounds. I hesitated to tell Jimmy's story because I didn't know what to say.

His life was a mess. He didn't like himself, but in dying he reinforced a belief I had learned years ago, something he never grasped. It really is okay to love yourself. How can you possibly love anyone else if you don't?

When Jesus was asked which is the most important commandment, He answered, "'Love the Lord your God with all your heart and with all your soul and with all your mind.' This is the first and greatest commandment. And the second is like it: 'Love your neighbor *as yourself.*' All the law and the Prophets hang on these two commandments" (Matt. 22:35–40, italics added). I believe that when we embrace what this passage says, it changes the way we perceive life. We won't go around plotting ways to get our neighbors' goods, nor will we set out to hurt anyone.

Uncle Johnnie tried to help Jimmy. Uncle Lloyd and Aunt Ruthie tried too. But Jimmy couldn't or wouldn't help himself. He was the saddest person I have ever known.

CHAPTER 46

Farewell to a Friend

Our last goodbye to our friends Paul and Yvonne Tribel was particularly difficult and special. They were heading back to Australia after one of our holidays together. Ed and I accompanied them to the airport.

As I hugged and kissed Yvonne, something in my spirit sensed that would be the last time I would see her. I hung on to her and cried my heart out. She did the same.

As we were walking away, I told Ed, "I'll never see her again." When Paul called us and told us that Yvonne was dead, I wasn't surprised, although I was grief stricken. Through the loss of his wife, Paul found a closer walk with God.

We had a wonderful friendship, and I treasure every moment. I understood Yvonne, and she knew what was in my heart. I knew our relationship was a gift.

I'll see Yvonne again someday when I get to heaven. She'll be in my welcoming party. She'll be even more beautiful than when she was on earth. She'll be the tall, stately one with the million-dollar smile.

CHAPTER 47

The Chosen People

I looked up Eddie and Erica Ausch from Reisner's Delicatessen to thank them for being so good to me when I was down and out. They were happy to know that I hadn't forgotten them. Then they accepted a dinner invitation to my house! Finally, I had a chance to cook for them. We had a glorious evening.

A week or so later, Erica called and invited Ed and me to their house for dinner. I was thrilled!

After a delicious meal (real Hungarian goulash), we got reacquainted. So much has happened since we knew each other more than thirty years ago. Now retired, they love to travel when they aren't babysitting. Erica has pictures of her grandchildren in the kitchen. I do that!

She told me all about her daughters and grandchildren. Daughter Jodie works in a health food store. I didn't know I had been seeing her for a few years. She has two children, Leo and Liza. Linda opened a Reisner's Delicatessen near the resort area of Virginia Beach. She is carrying on her family's good name. They were known and respected for excellence throughout the Norfolk and Virginia Beach communities. Bonnie is happily married with two children, Blake and Raven. Eddie had a stroke just before Bonnie planned to be married. He was so determined to walk his daughter down the isle that he pressed on and made it. They had to hold him up, but he was there, and Bonnie had a beautiful wedding.

Uncle Leo, with the devilish eyes, died in a funny way, if dying can be funny. On Thanksgiving Day he was sitting in his easy chair, all dressed up in suit and tie—dead. Gone. Passed away. On the other side. He went out with style, just as he had lived. He will be remembered with a smile.

After dinner, Eddie and Erica shared some things that touched me. While they were children in Austria, their families were displaced when Hitler's army marched through Europe. Erica was only two years old, but naturally she had heard stories from her parents. They had to live on a barge floating around, waiting for a relative to send them a voucher stating that they would have employment in Norfolk, Virginia. Mr. Reisner had been a businessman, but he and his family had walked away from everything. Because of their strength of spirit, his family lived and prospered. Because of their sacrifice, Erica is here today. Anyone who knows her, loves her.

Eddie was older during the Holocaust, so he remembers. He is definitely not passive about his memories; he's like me—very "cheeky." Eddie says he isn't as nice as he use to be. But I don't believe it.

We learn history and see current world atrocities on television and in books and magazines, but it is still so hard to believe that something as awful as the Holocaust actually happened—and could, God help us, happen again. The horror became more real to me through these caring human beings.

Besides being compassionate and good, Eddie and Erica really know how to make any meal a feast. To me, part of the fun of living is enjoying the blessings God has given us. The Jewish people know how to do that in the grandest way. No wonder God chose them. I'd choose them too!

CHAPTER 48

Hands Reaching Out

Somewhere in my travels, I lost Caroline's address. I was worried and couldn't get her off my mind. I had a recurring dream. Lying on a hospital bed, Caroline was covered with a white sheet. Her hand was reaching out from under the cover, and she was calling my name.

One day while I was cleaning, I thought about one of Granddaddy's silly songs, "Joe Blow from Idaho." Then I remembered that Caroline had a brother-in-law named Joe Blow. I wondered, *How many Joe Blows could there be?* There were two in the directory.

Bingo! Joe Blow number one recognized my voice and remembered my name. He said, "Yes, Billie, I know you; you're Caroline's friend." He gave me Caroline's sister Mae's telephone number.

I trembled when Mae told me that Caroline had cancer and had just undergone a mastectomy. She said my friend was in Arkansas and gave me her number.

Dear God, could it possibly be that my dear friend had needed me for a change? I called down a band of angels for my best friend, just as she had called them down for me time and time again. I had to compose myself before I could dial the number.

When she heard my voice, Caroline yelled, "Oh, Billie, girl! Oh girl!" She praised God and thanked Jesus about a million times before we settled down. Yes, she had been thinking of me.

Just when I thought I could do something for her, she gave me another lesson in faith. She was sure that God would restore the glow of health to her body. She said, "The Lord is good."

To make myself feel better, I said, "God loves you girl, and I love you. I'm holding your hand. I won't *ever* let you go."

Caroline and Charles live in Norfolk now. He retired from the air force. Charlotte and Charles, Jr. are grown and on their own. They are both credits to their parents. Caroline worked hard and spent every cent she made, sending her children to private schools. She taught them how to live by her shining example.

Our Christmas feast is blessed with their presence at our table. This year for Christmas, she gave her husband a memory calendar. Each month displays a favorite picture. The December photo shows the four of us—Charles, Caroline, Ed, and me—in front of our Christmas tree.

> Hands touching hands, reaching out
> Touching you, touching me
> Sweet Caroline . . .[1]

I know for certain that I could not have been blessed with a better friend. When my family gathers around the pianola on Christmas Eve, the celebration wouldn't be as joyous without my lifelong friend. The sweet pure tones of her voice rise up and ring out the news: "Christ the Savior is born, Christ the Savior is born."

I believe it, girl. I believe it.

Section V.
Nothing is Impossible

CHAPTER 49

Mother-and-Child Reunion

Volumes have been written about mother-daughter relationships, but where were they when I needed them? More than likely, I was too mixed up to get through the first chapter.

My Pattie was such a sweet bundle of joy as a baby. The time passed too quickly. Before I knew it, she was answering the telephone and saying, "Who needs it?"—her childish version of "Who is it?"

When she folded her little arms across her chest, stomped her foot, and said, "Own self," I knew we would go around a few times. It was a test of motherhood that I would fail—miserably. My daughter, like her mother, has been through one trauma after another.

Someday we will have a mother-and-child reunion filled with joy and love. Until then, all I can do is trust in God's plan for her and for me.

Today, Pattie and the love of her life, Tom, are married and live in Michigan. It took awhile for her to see and understand that before she could truly love him, she had to love herself. Tom was patient and kind. He saw her beauty which was buried under all the pain she had been carrying around since childhood. She is a writer, teacher, and entrepreneur. My daughter has always been artistic and creative. She churns out glass beads, paintings, sculpture, and her own line of clothing. Her work shows a love of all things ethnic. She has five videos on the market in beadmaking. I am very proud of her achievements. More importantly, I am proud of her and the woman she is becoming. She calls herself Trisha now. But she will always be my Summer, my Fall, my Winter, my Spring.

. . . .

CHAPTER 50

Dreams You
Dare to Dream

T he first time I saw my granddaughter, Sara, she was three months old. My heart was racing. She looked just like me without the jug ears. I could hardly believe the resemblance. Thank God she was the firstborn. The middle child syndrome won't affect her.

Soon after my daughter-in-law, Kathie, went back to work, Sara started getting sick with every germ that blew her way. Kathie and Eddy were frantic. I was so proud of Kathie when she quit the job that she had loved for eight years. She made an unselfish decision. She is the answer to my prayers for Eddy. Kathie said that it would be difficult for her and Eddy. They wouldn't be able to afford a better house or a new car. I told her that children don't care where they live, as long as they are loved. What they really need is parents who care.

Sara has been in and out of the hospital more times than most hypochondriacs. The poor child has no immune system to fight off invading bacteria. By the time she gets built up, she's right back in the hospital. She knows more medical terms than I do and can tell you what the doctors will do next.

After Wesley Aaron was born, it was difficult trying to handle everything. Eddy sounded worried about his family, and he was working so hard. I went to South Carolina to help out and take some of the pressure off Kathie. My granddaughter was hollow-eyed and frail. Hooked up to an IV, Sara seemed so small in her hospital bed.

I was thrilled when Kathie said I could stay all night and take her place. Sara asked if I wanted to watch her favorite movie with her. Old Nanny smiled all over herself when Sara held up her very own copy of *The Wizard of Oz*.

"That's my all-time favorite movie too," I told Sara, and we both laughed.

We sang "Somewhere Over the Rainbow" together. She knew every word of the movie, and she was two-and-one-half years old.

After she was released from the hospital, we made cookies. Sara is a wonderful cookie decorator. Her specialty is applying sprinkles. We discussed the possibility of opening up a cookie shop. She sees, "SARA and Nanny's Little Cookie Shop." I see "Nanny and Sara's Shop." We might have a few kinks to work out. Wesley would like to be our official cookie taster. He is extremely dedicated.

Not even a month later, Sara was back in the hospital. When I arrived, she was sitting on the bed, holding her stuffed animal, Pinky. She said, "Hi, Nanny," and her little face lit right up. I wanted to cry. We just had to watch Dorothy again.

During that hospital stay, I was allowed to accompany Sara to the x ray department for an MRI. A lovely lady took Sara down the hall in a little red wagon. Sara captured everyone's hearts, with her golden blonde curls shining under the lights. Everyone remarked how beautiful her curls were. I said I loved my granddaughter so much that I had given them to her so that she would never forget me. She said, "Oh, silly Nanny. My daddy gave me my curls."

When we arrived at the x ray room, Sara started to tense up. I told her I was an expert on that kind of thing and could tell her all about what was happening. All they wanted to do was take a real close look at her head. The only thing she had to remember was to be very still so the pictures would be clear. It would not hurt one single bit, and I would stand right next to her and hold her hand. Not only that, but I would pinch anybody who tried to tell me to leave. God bless her heart, she didn't move a muscle, but she sure was squeezing Nanny's hand.

Sara had so many sinus infections that the scars were clearly visible. The prescribed course of treatment was more antibiotics and an inhaler four times a day.

To complicate matters more for my son's family, Wesley was born with acid reflux and asthma. Kathie administers Maalox to coat his stomach and neutralize the acid. The dear little fellow recently stayed five days in the hospital for bacterial pneumonia. My son and daughter-in-law took it all in stride and dealt with it.

Wesley inherited my feet. They are square, brick-shaped, pudgy little things. His mother has difficulty finding shoes for him. I find the quality endearing.

Wesley is confused about his future vocation. He can't decide if he wants to be a tool man or a farmer. I hope all of his dreams come true. He has a mommy and daddy who will be right there to help him build a bridge to any dream in his heart.

I have written two stories about "Wesley the Wonder Boy." The first one begins:

It wasn't because he could tear a telephone book in half or jump higher than his sister, Sara, that gave Nanny the idea to call him Wesley the Wonder Boy. It was simply because Wesley liked to wonder. He wondered about everything. He sometimes looked up in the sky and wondered how it would feel if he could fly with the birds. His Grandpapa Jim had an airplane of his own and told little Wesley that one day he would take him on an airplane ride. Then he would even be able to see the tops of houses and clouds. Wesley thought that it might take him forever to grow up. He wondered if he flapped his arms fast enough, could he fly all by himself?

The story goes on to describe Wesley's delightful never-ending curiosities. The child is a genius, there's no doubt about it. He is above average in intelligence, just like his sister. It's in the genes; that's what I tell Eddy. Wesley is simply taking after his Pa. Eddy loved to take things apart. Remember the eye story? Yes, it's just natural curiosity.

Eddy is a carpenter. He has his own business in Greenville, South Carolina. He is getting a reputation that says he's honest and will give you his best. Eddy is a people-person with a winning way and a beautiful smile. To Eddy, a stranger is just a friend he hasn't met yet.

My son also has his own line of patio furniture. I love what he has done to their house. He built a wraparound deck, which Kathie loves. They have swings and chairs and planters for flowers. The kids can play outside while Kathie checks on them easily from the windows.

I always knew Eddy was gifted. He writes his own songs and plays the guitar. He taught himself shortly after his father passed away. He just picked up a guitar one day and started playing. It was almost second nature.

I never could bring myself to tell Eddy that he inherited the middle child syndrome from his mother. He still thinks that he was just maladjusted. I'm hoping that when he reads this book he will forgive me for letting him wonder about himself. He was simply following his genetic code.

Eddy has developed into a loving, caring man, and I am so proud. I believe his spirit heard me when I crept into his room so many years ago and whispered in his ear, "You are good and you are loved." God took that message to the heart of a little boy who didn't get much praise for the wonderful things that he did. Those words stuck in a place where the devil himself couldn't go. The angels wouldn't allow it.

CHAPTER 51

The Still, Small Voice

O ne of my life's greatest pleasures is visiting my son Larry. Ed
refers to him as my "personal guru and all-time gimcrack king."
A gimcrack is any useless trinket or thingamajig that you can't
live without; it may sparkle, beep, light up, talk, or just lay in your hand
and do nothing. Whatever it does or doesn't do, you must have it. Larry
has a wide variety of gimcracks and enjoys every one of them. He knows
they are useless, but he doesn't care what people think or say. That's the
universal code of all of those who collect and covet gimcracks.

Larry lives in Lacey Spring, Virginia, in a little cottage alongside the
main road, and he is perhaps the wisest person I know. It is to him I go
for advice and guidance. I love being with him. We can talk half the
night about our mutual interests. Then after he goes to work, I enjoy
looking at and organizing his gimcracks. He is patient and doesn't fuss
too much if he can't find something. He has rows and rows of interesting books. We both enjoy watching his stacks of old movies that he
finds at flea markets and Goodwill stores. Larry is a good person. He
always finds someone in need of something. God bless his giving heart.
The song I bequeath to him is "You're the Best Thing that Ever Happened to Me." It was because of my love for him that I stepped outside
myself and saw the needs of someone else.

If anyone should ever write my life story,
For whatever reason there might be,
You'd be there between each line
Of pain and glory,
'Cause you're the best thing
That ever happened to me. . . .[1]

Larry's life took a dramatic change for the better several years ago. I was in the waiting room of Dr. David McDaniel when I noticed a print of the song "Amazing Grace" on the wall. Always a favorite of mine, I read each line and reflected on God's grace in my own life. From out of the blue, I had this thought: *He is the one who will help you with your son Larry.* It seemed strange since I was there for my own benefit. Again, like a whisper, the message spoke softly in my mind: *He is the one who will help you with your son Larry.*

Where this thought would lead me, I didn't have a clue. I did know that it was up to me to at least mention my son to the doctor. I have learned that nothing significant happens by chance. When God's timing is right, He lets us know, and it's up to us to step out in faith.

When my name was called, the nurse directed me to an examining room. When I met Dr. McDaniel for the first time, I liked him right away. He had a wonderful way of putting a new patient at ease. After we discussed what had brought me to him, I casually mentioned my son.

I explained Larry's defects as briefly as I could. Then I mentioned the psychological ramifications Larry encountered in dealing with the birth defects throughout his life. I told him about the anguish and rejection that had been a constant part of Larry's earliest memories, beginning with hurtful remarks and the stares of other children. His despair had carried over through adolescence and into manhood as he was subjected to the unfairness of lost employment opportunities. As a young man, he stood by and watched romantic relationships pass him by.

When I had finished telling Dr. McDaniel these things, he invited me to bring Larry in. I could sense he was interested, but I didn't want to press.

Over the next few weeks, I couldn't get Larry off my mind. He was thirty-two and working in a poultry processing plant in Harrisonburg, Virginia. Prior to that, he had prepared vegetables and done janitorial work in a local restaurant. He had completed two years of college. He is very bright and contains so much potential, but because of his facial deformities, many doors were closed to him. He once wrote beautiful poetry to the girl of his dreams and wondered if he would ever find her. About five years prior, he had left flowers and a card on the car of a young lady he cared for, only to be ridiculed and laughed at. Dispirited, he gave up on romance and buried himself in his books. He loves God's Word and devotes many hours to studying Hebrew and Greek.

On my next visit to Dr. McDaniel, the thought occurred again. *He is the one who will help you with your son Larry.* I recalled that in my first conversation with the doctor concerning Larry, he had asked if I knew that he was the director for the Center for Facial Disfigurement. I had replied, "No," but I thought, *God surely knew it.*

I had told Dr. McDaniel that Larry didn't have much money, and he really needed someone to help him. Dr. McDaniel gave me a pamphlet about his clinic. He said to send some close-up pictures of Larry's face to him. I had skipped out of his office filled with hope.

I decided to wait until I thought it was the right time to tell Larry about Dr. McDaniel. Larry had undergone so many painful procedures, but they hadn't achieved much. Doctors had done what they could when my son was a small boy, but plastic surgery was a relatively new field thirty years ago, and laser surgery was unheard of. I had to be careful in suggesting that more surgery might help him.

Everything came together when I called Larry and asked him if he still wanted the pickup truck I had promised him. I drove up to Harrisonburg to get him. While driving back to my house in Virginia Beach, I told him about Dr. McDaniel. I said I wasn't sure what it all meant, yet I felt confident that good would come of it. He agreed to the close-up photos.

When the photos were developed, I wrote a lengthy letter to Dr. McDaniel, which I personally delivered, pouring my heart out. A week later I received a very encouraging letter from him, explaining that there was a strong possibility that Larry could be helped. He had forwarded my letter and photos to a plastic surgeon in Norfolk. I knew then that life would change for Larry, and it happened sooner than I ever imagined.

A few days later, I received a call from Dr. James Carraway, who wanted to know all about Larry. His voice revealed that he was a caring person who truly wanted to help us. We talked for about twenty minutes. I told him about the artificial eye that had been made for my son many years ago, which was too big and heavy and had, in the course of time, made the eye sag. I explained that Larry's misshapen left nostril added further distortion to that side of his face and that his one ear, being an inch lower than the other, made his face appear lopsided. Dr. Carraway said that he thought he could help us. When he hung up, I couldn't contain the hope and joy in my heart. I cried happy tears and thanked God for His amazing grace. Dr. Carraway's secretary called right back to schedule an appointment.

In July 1996 we met Dr. Carraway. He treated Larry with great care, and I was moved by the doctor's obvious compassion. He asked my son to explain his feelings about his facial defects and what concerned him the most about his appearance. Larry spoke of his lifelong struggle in such a touching personal way that it was all I could do to keep my composure. I heard the anguish in his voice; I felt his pain.

Dr. Carraway left us for a moment, and I told my son how proud I was of him. The doctor returned to inform us that Larry's insurance would cover the cost of surgery in and around his eye socket. However, the procedures needed to repair Larry's ear and nose were considered cosmetic and not covered. Dr. Carraway said he would not charge us for those costly procedures. He then gave us the name of an oculist who would make Larry's new eye. We set a surgery date.

We were ecstatic! Larry and I hugged each other in the elevator. We had never met anyone so kind and unselfish; we had so much to be thankful for.

At 6:00 a.m., November 18, 1996, we checked into the hospital. Dr. Carraway made a series of marks on Larry's face and ear. Despite our anxiety, he made us feel comfortable. We knew we were in good hands and that God was with us. Soon after, attendants came to take my son to the operating room. I kissed him and said, "I love you, Larry. Very soon I'll be seeing a new you."

Four hours later, Dr. Carraway entered the waiting room and explained the operation to me. He had taken a graft from Larry's leg to build up the area around his eye. He had reshaped the ear and used the tissue from the lobe to balance the left nostril. He cautioned that procedures done to the nose would be difficult to heal and that prayers would help. I told him that all my friends and three churches were praying for Larry.

When I was allowed into the recovery room, I was overwhelmed by the difference. Tears rolled down my cheeks. All I could manage to say before Larry fell back to sleep was, "Oh, Larry!" For me to be speechless is monumental. I stepped back to look at my sleeping son. Even through the blood, I could see that his eye sockets were level in position and equal in size. His ears were balanced, and his nose was beautiful. It was a miracle far beyond my expectations! My son would never have to hide in the shadows from anything or anyone ever again.

Three days later we returned to see Dr. Carraway. He couldn't believe how quickly the tissue was healing. The nose graft looked so good he was able to remove most of the stitches. Our prayers had been heard. Dr. Carraway was kind enough to tell us that he always prays to God before surgery and asks Him to guide and direct his hands. We thanked him and God from the bottom of our hearts.

One week later, we tested the new look. Larry and I went to the nursing home where I volunteer. I wanted him to meet the old dears who had been praying for him. Helen Harris, a sweet soul of ninety-three, threw up her arms and cried out, "Larry!" when she saw him. They held each other, and she said, "I've been praying so hard for you." He looked deep into her eyes and thanked her for her prayers and concern for him. I could see that Larry was visibly shaken. He needed to know about the kindness of strangers. It was made clear to him that people like Helen really do care and want to give whatever they have.

We walked up and down the halls of the nursing home. Not one person pointed, stared, or whispered. Larry was just an ordinary guy visiting some friends. For the first time in his life, no one noticed him because of the way he looked.

We visited his grandmother on the way home. She noticed that he held his shoulders straighter and his head higher. It was quite a transformation.

Thanks to the amazing grace of God, we had a wonderful Thanksgiving at my house. God had led me to Dr. McDaniel, who had been moved by a mother's plea and had referred us to a trusted colleague. Dr. Carraway's unselfish kindness touched us and made a life-changing difference. We will always be grateful to him for his wonderful gift. Now the door of possibility is open for Larry. What he does with the marvelous opportunity can be his gift in return.

A real miracle happened for my son and me. It began in a waiting room. We all have the power to tune in to that still small voice inside us. We can step out in faith, as I did, or turn away and miss something beautiful. Faith is the key to finding miracles, and prayer is the force that opens the door for anyone who dares to believe.

It never ceases to amaze me how forgiving my son is to me. I can't help but remember how patient he was as I dragged him to every lecture, church, or meeting where the guest speaker had some kind of handicap. It didn't matter to me what kind. If they could speak and had made any kind of life for themselves, we were there.

"See there, Son," I'd encourage, "if he or she can do it, you can do it too."

Every time one of the "beautiful" people died tragically, he had to listen to my sermon about beauty being skin deep and of no use to whoever had just died.

"What good did all those looks do them, huh?" I'd ask.

The world told Larry something entirely different. The great society said, "If you aren't pretty, we don't want you." The biggest obstacle in the kid's life was his own mother. And he loved me anyway.

He survived in spite of everything, and, God bless him, he's reaching out to others who are in need of encouragement. He is saying, "If I can make it, you can make it." His personal testimony is much more convincing than mine will ever be. I am so proud of him I could jump up and down.

Larry has recently been given a grant to continue his education. This summer he is going to a small community college in Harrisonburg. He wants to study therapeutic massage and herbal medicine. He has taken and passed the test for employment with the United States Postal Service. He's considering starting as a part-time rural letter carrier and working his way up. In the meantime, he is now working in the hatchery instead of the processing plant, where it is so terribly cold. In the hatchery, it is nice and warm and his feet and hands don't hurt anymore.

It is a joyous thing to see him with his head held high. Watching him grow and become a loving, tenderhearted person truly is the best thing that ever happened to me. Whatever the future holds for Larry, I know he'll be successful because God has His eye on him.

CHAPTER 52

. . . .

Poems and Prayers

S adly, I don't know where my son Steven is, and I haven't seen him in a few years. I will tell you what I know.

As a baby, he won a baby contest. He was a beautiful child.

He is a writer. His poems are wonderfully mysterious and filled with symbolism.

He loves the sea. He might be sailing somewhere or fishing in the Chesapeake Bay. He likes rockfish.

Steven is also a musician and finds comfort in his music.

He enjoys gardening and has a natural knack for nurturing green things. There is something inside of him that loves to see things grow.

When he was a small boy, he designed a better mousetrap. It scared all the mice away.

Steven is very handsome and has my pudgy feet and curly hair.

Someday he will be able to see me as someone who loves him rather than someone who failed him. God's ways are perfect. The timing isn't right yet. Maybe it will be tomorrow.

Until that happy day, I will keep his picture in my room and pray that he is well and finding joy in life. I will always have his song. I can take it out of my heart and sing the lyrics:

You'd be like heaven to touch. . . .
I want to hold you so much. . . .[1]

CHAPTER 53

Ninety-six Cans of Olives

E d should never have retired. Out of all the crazy things I've experienced in my life, it may be his incessant coupon clipping that finally drives me bonkers! Sunday is the worst day of the week. Ed wakes up dizzy with anticipation and whistles as he races to get the newspaper. He searches with one thought on his mind, *Will there be one or two brilliantly colored inserts in the paper today?* There is joy in our home if he finds a dollar-off, special, one-time-only kind of deal.

Wednesday is also a terrible day, because the food section of our Wednesday paper has the weekly bargain sections for all our local supermarkets. The Farmer Jack song that plays throughout the store Ed frequents most often is not one of his all-time favorite tunes, but he doesn't care what he has to subject himself to on his eternal quest to save twenty cents. According to Ed, coupons are a veritable windfall of savings. He is wildly happy if his Sunday coupons complement his Wednesday coupons.

My husband claims he never pays more than six cents for a bar of soap. We have over a hundred bars. And we have ninety-six cans of olives. We use three, maybe four, cans of olives per year. I do like olives, but I think ninety-six cans is excessive.

Ed needs help; however, he is in denial. Surely there must be a chapter of "coupon clippers anonymous" somewhere. I suggested that he establish a chapter if necessary; it might be a saving grace for others with the same vexation of spirit. If he could hear himself say, "Hello, my name is Ed; I have ninety-six cans of olives"; it might put him on the road to recovery. I have difficulty watching my commander in the United States Navy on an intense quest to save on the grocery bill. Shouldn't he be out somewhere commanding something? Or helping to solve the world's problems or planning some military strategy—anything other than driving me to the moon.

Our home has five thousand square feet of living space. Every closet, drawer, and storage unit is filled with stuff. Ed claims you can't have too many napkins, paper towels, or rolls of toilet paper. At last count, we had fifty-eight economy size jars of spaghetti sauce. I make my own. We have enough tea bags to take us through the next ten years, even if we consumed a frosty pitcher full of iced tea every day.

The cabinets in our summer home are also filled to capacity with canned goods, shampoo, deodorant, and sardines. The storage closet in our laundry room is frightening. There are so many cans and spray bottles of cleaning compounds, that if you try to remove one, ten fall on your head. The chance of avalanche is far too dangerous for a short person like me. I should wear a helmet if I am forced to brave it alone.

Both of our freezers are filled. Still, I can't find anything. My packing skills are not up to Ed's level. I always end up with more stuff than I can possibly jam back in.

The one redeeming element in this whole coupon thing is that Ed and I will never starve. When I complain, his children snicker, with a knowing look in their eyes. This is not a new thing.

Ed's daughter, Debi, and I share a lot of laughs over Ed's obsessive-compulsive behavior that, according to his children, goes way back. Debi says that her father had two closets for his storehouse of stuff when she was a child—one for him and one for them.

His son Steve knows how I feel. We relate well with each other. As children, Steve and I were both stuck in the middle. There was no use trying to compete with the saintly firstborn. And we weren't the cuddly babies. There's goodness inside of Steve that makes him easy to talk to.

The youngest of the three is brave enough to laugh and tell his father straight out that he has rocks in his head. He sees the endless supply of everything as pretty ridiculous and says so. Scott doesn't mince words. Everybody in our neighborhood appreciates him. He has his own landscaping business and keeps our lawns looking like magazine photos. He has a great ability in visualizing how flowerbeds and shrubs should compliment a home and then making it real. He's the most hardworking fellow I have ever met.

Ed's children didn't know what to think when I came on the scene. It took a while for them to see that we could be friends. Sometimes I feel sorry for all our grown children, his and mine. When we both die, it will take them forever to go through our belongings in both of our houses. The toilet paper alone could take days to divide. I can't help but wonder: *Who will get the olives?*

In all fairness, I have to say there are many blessings in my life with Ed. For instance, his son Scott's wife, Shirl (nee Shirley Marie Craig), is *my* daughter-in-law. Before she even conceived her children, she asked if I would be a grandmother to her offspring. The granny in me shouted, "Would I? Of course! And God bless your sweet heart for allowing me the privilege."

When Shirl discovered that she would need a fertility expert, I applauded her. Together we went through her surgery because of endometriosis. I held her hand and never once heard her complain about the pain. I marveled at her determination when she had to inject herself with a fertility drug. My soul truly rejoiced when she conceived.

I cried and prayed all the way to the hospital after someone had called to tell me that my daughter-in-law had been in an accident and was asking for me. That was the longest ride in the world. When I saw her, I saw my own child sitting in a wheelchair, and it was very difficult to be brave for her. The machines looked new and threatening to me, but Shirl was eager to know what was happening to her and her babies. God bless her maternal heart, she rubbed her tummy and said, "Mommy is here. Don't worry; we'll be all right." Baby A and Baby B, as the hospital staff referred to her twins, waved and flipped, obviously shaken, as was their mommy. She was unable to hold back her tears at the sight of them on the monitor. Their little heartbeats pounded; they were not in danger. Their little waving arms told me, "Don't cry, Nanny, We're all shook up, but we are going to make it." Katia Marie and Marshall Edward were born two months ahead of schedule on December 31, 1996.

Katia, whom we call Katie, is one minute older. She has flashing brown eyes, olive skin, and tulip lips. Sometimes she is K.T. or Katie Girl. She responds to anything spoken with love, especially if you are holding a cookie.

Marshall Edward is blonde with blue-gray eyes and fair complexion, like me. Katie came home from the hospital first because she was stronger, although Marshall was slightly larger.

Ed and I sat with Katie when her mommy and daddy went to get her brother. Ed, or "Poppy" as he likes to be called by his grandchildren, cried when he held her. When I asked her if she missed the angels, she smiled so big that I had to cry too. When we put Marshall in the crib with his sister, she reached out and touched his face as if to say, "Where have you been?" We have that documented in a photo which still makes me cry.

Shirl had to return to work shortly before the babies were six weeks old, to continue her medical benefits. We were the babysitters. For six months, we diapered, stroked, rocked, and fed the twins. The bonding that took place was incredibly strong.

Katie is going to be a force to reckon with because of her independent nature and rock-solid will. I get the biggest kick out of watching her stiffen her legs and howl when she expresses displeasure.

I wrote a poem for our Katie.

Katie
Forget the dishes Nanny, we haven't very long.
I'm growing oh so fast these days and someday, I'll be gone.
Who knows what will become of me as I travel on my way?
The ground for my tomorrows will be cast in yesterdays.
The cares of living all remain, but right now, Nanny dear,
We'll play dress-up, or maybe house, and you can brush my hair.
The dust will be there and the chores; I can't see them anyway.
I see your smile, I feel your love with every passing day.
My feet have such a long, long way to go 'til I am grown.
Show me where the path is that I must walk alone.
Teach me with your actions what you really value most,
And when you cuddle up with me, Nanny, hold me close.
In moments of pure solitude when I am old and gray,
I'll lean back on those memories of happy childhood days.
This world can be a bitter place, the angels told me so.
They also mentioned you'd be here with shelter from the cold.

Every word you've said to me is written on my heart.
I remember how you welcomed me right from the very start.
You asked me if I missed the angels far away,
And thanked God for the gift of me into your family.
It felt so warm and safe there, when you were holding me.
I saw the tears there in your eyes. You said, "I'm your Nanny."
I came from heaven. My name is Katie,
Nanny. My Nanny was waiting for me.

Marshall is a tender, sweet child. My dearest memory of him will always be the day he sang the "Barney" song to me, and only me.

I wrote a poem for our Marshall too.

Little Boy Boo
Little Boy Boo, come play with me. . . .
"What can we do to have fun today? I know, I know," said Marshall,
Who's two, "We'll play hide and seek, and I will say 'Boooooooooo!'"
It started long before he knew
What's a cow, what's a bird, and just what is a Boo?
They could scarcely believe it when Nanny told them it's true,
"Besides 'Ma Ma' and 'Da Da,' the child can say 'Boo.'"
Tucked safely in his baby bed, she put his blankie on his head;
Lifting it off, Nanny smiled and said "Boo!"
Marshall from heaven soon learned what to do.
She'll never forget the look of surprise,
The mischief and merriment there in his eyes.
Angel baby began to crawl. He hid around corners and waited so
Still. She found him, she found him, she always knew
Just where to look for her Little Boy Boo.
Scooping him up in her arms with care,
Laughing and giggling, she tousled his hair.
"I see you! I see you! I see you there!"
Falling and wobbling, but making great strides,
He found a zillion places to hide.
Behind a couch or under a bed,
She drew him out and kissed his sweet head.
He grew and he climbed and discovered new spaces,
But he never outgrew his Nanny's embraces.
He won't stay a baby; someday he'll be grown.
One day he may have a dear boy of his own.

Whatever happens, whatever comes true, when she looks back with
Fondness and happiness too,
She'll thank God for the memories of Little Boy Boo.
Little Boy Boo, come play with me. . . .

When we aren't playing with the babies, we are traveling on "free" military air transport flights to anywhere we can go. Last year it was Sigonella, Sicily, for two weeks, and then up the "boot" all the way to Venice, Italy, which took my breath away. We had a flash run through all of the major attractions along the way.

While at a small army base, Camp Elderly, in Vincenza, Ed said he wanted to go to the commissary and get some luncheon meat for our trip back to Sigonella. Since I can't possibly keep up with him in a grocery store, I said I would hang out at the exchange and look at the Italian scarves. While sitting at a table by the cafeteria, I saw a young woman who resembled my nephew Joe's wife, Donisa. I said, "Excuse me, but is your name Donisa?"

Here eyes nearly bugged out of her head. "Aunt Billie, what are you doing here?"

I explained the situation and asked if my nephew was anywhere around. In less than five minutes, my own dear nephew, Joseph A. Hughes, Jr., and I were hugging and kissing each other right there in Italy. I saw him running across the parking lot, grinning like a child, and I ran to him and jumped right on him, wrapping my legs around his waist. I was so happy to see him.

Joe told me that when Donisa said, "You'll never believe who is sitting outside the exchange," he, of course, thought that it had to be his adventurous Aunt Billie. The good Lord knew that if I had been that close to my nephew and missed seeing him that my heart would never get over the disappointment. Not only that, but Joe needed to see me to soothe his soul. That dear young man was parted from our family many years ago and sometimes still feels separated. I knew that Joe was somewhere in Italy, but his mailing address is an army post office box number. Who can explain what happened without thinking that a higher power is more in control of our lives than we can imagine? All the players had to be in the right place at the exact time. Only God could have accomplished such an extraordinary meeting.

The Leaning Tower of Pisa is still leaning, and the statue of David is the most beautiful piece of marble I have ever seen. We found Italians to be very passionate people, especially behind the wheel of a car. The number-one rule for motorists is: never look the other drivers in the eye. They will run over you, kill you if they have to. After they destroy your vehicle, they will invite you to a spaghetti dinner.

Ed is an excellent tour guide. He has an uncanny way of finding terrific tourist spots and then finding our way back to our hotel. It boggles my mind. I get lost in Virginia Beach, where I have lived for over forty years. He knows where north is by sniffing the air. It's almost inhuman.

When I first met Ed, he told me to stick with him, and he would have me wearing silk and traveling the world. I do like to travel. Seeing Paris was a dream come true for me. While we were there, we met up with Ed's brother, David, who was in France on business. At that time, he represented General Electric at Euro-Disneyland. David took us there as his guests. We had a fabulous time. I got to see Tweedle Dee and Tweedle Dum in France.

While on my maiden voyage to Europe, we sailed across the Irish Sea to the land of my forefathers. We discovered the joys of the bed-and-breakfast method of accommodations. I highly recommend this style of touring, because you meet very interesting people around the breakfast table.

When in Ireland, you also get to hear the quaint language of your Irish host or hostess. Hearing them speak is like listening to music. I did kiss the Blarney Stone. At that very moment, the gift of eloquence was bestowed upon me by the powers that be. I have a certificate to prove it. Ed would not kiss the stone. He said no self-respecting Pole would stoop to that silly, pointless custom.

I was shocked to see the visible proof of my ancestry in the huge ears of the general population of Ireland. There was no getting around it; they are my people. It was all I could do to refrain from shouting my regrets for plastic surgery. If I had left my jug ears alone, my countrymen would have seen the visible proof of our kinship. But, alas, I was just another tourist.

The highlands of Scotland were beautiful in every way. We also have Scottish relations on my family tree. And, yes indeed, the Hughes ears were represented everywhere. We stayed in a resort not far from the

Birks of Aberfeldy, where Robert Burns penned his famous poem with the same name. No wonder he was so inspired—the beauty of the Birks is enough to move any soul to compose. We surely walked in the famed poet's footsteps at the falls. I did not eat haggis in Aberfeldy.

All things considered, I think I am more British than anything else. I do like the pomp and circumstance. It's all so regal. I even enjoyed high tea at the Savoy Hotel in London. We got all dressed up to the nines and sat with other tourists in the hotel lobby. We all sipped tea and sampled finger sandwiches from silver trays. I was amused at the others who were watching me, thinking I knew what I was doing. I was immensely proud of myself for not spilling one morsel or drooling on my clothing. London was the highlight of England. We must have seen every major theatre production, including *The Phantom of the Opera* (I was giddy for weeks after that) and the unforgettable *Les Miserables*.

We stopped in to see our friends May and Ken Brisley in Hillhead, Fareham. Ken and Ed were stationed in Australia at the same time. He and his wife, May, named their house "Trees" because of the lovely trees in their backyard. I wanted to see an English country garden, and Ken was happy to show off his handiwork. I don't know why anyone would say the British are dull. Ken Brisley is the funniest man I know. He has a clever way of sneaking a hilarious joke into a conversation. Then he sits with a devilish smile, waiting for his audience to get it. He will laugh with you until your sides ache.

May is a sweet lady. She loves to reminisce about her life as a secretary to a lovable, but often tipsy lawyer. The poor man couldn't hide his bottle from May. We took a day trip with the Brisleys to Plymouth, England. It was wonderful seeing where the courageous pilgrims had set sail for the new land called America. I wish we could have stayed with our friends a bit longer, but we had many places to visit.

While we were strolling in St. James Park, in London, I saw an old man sitting on a park bench fiddling with something. He was busy drawing in his sketchbook when I invaded his space. At that time, George Emmerson was eighty years young. He always sits in the same location, hoping someone will come along and talk to him. He has made friends from all over the world, just sitting in his little spot by the pond. We shared details of our lives, and he told me to keep doing whatever I am doing. He asked if he could hug me, and I felt very close to something beyond this earth in his embrace. He gave me an original watercolor and said if I would send him a postcard from home, he would send me another painting.

The first thing I did upon returning home was to mail a postcard to George. My new friend sent a beautiful painting of flowers in my favorite colors. I sent him a photo of our English Tudor home and invited him and his wife, Gladys, to Virginia. I cried like a baby when a package arrived with a painting of our home done from the small snapshot. It was an exact copy with perfect detail. Also enclosed was a painting of St. James Park, including the very place where Ed and I had met George. Ed and I were in the picture, strolling around the pond, just as we had done on that lovely day. The paintings are framed and proudly displayed for all who cross our threshold.

Now, If I could just figure out a way to meet face to face with the coal miner's daughter, Loretta Lynn, I would die a very happy Billie. I'd hug her and thank her for giving me songs to sing on rainy days. . . .

CHAPTER 54

That's Amore

Ed has known his best friend, Lynn Lilla, for approximately twelve years. They met on his last duty assignment with the Navy. Lynn was a master chief, the most proficient that Ed had ever worked with in his thirty-three-year career.

Ed had difficulty sorting out his feelings.

He told me he had never met any man that he cared as much for in his entire life. He loved his grandfather, father, brother, and sons—but this was different. Ed was in a quandary for days. I told him it was perfectly all right to admit that he loved Lynn. That did not mean that he wanted to run out and carve "Ed Loves Lynn" in a tree. The love between friends is priceless.

Anyone can see why Lynn is so lovable. He is warm, generous, trustworthy, and makes the best bread I have ever tasted. When we join them for dinner, he keeps that bread in the oven until everything is ready. When served, it is piping hot and delicious; I always eat too much. Lynn's Italian. To him it's no sin if anyone overindulges. In fact, I think Italian hosts are offended if you don't stuff yourself. Maybe Lynn could use some olives; it's just a thought.

If it were not for Lynn and his wife, Carol, Ed would not have had a retirement celebration. Lynn handled all the military preparations for the ceremony held on board the last ship Ed served aboard, the USS *Guadalcanal*. When Ed was "piped over the side," it was stirring. He saluted his country for the last time and left the ship with tears in his eyes. I had a few tears in my eyes too. No one looks better than Ed in a uniform. The party held at the Lilla's house afterward was fantastic. They worked so hard to make things nice for Ed. He deeply appreciated everything.

While I was taking care of Dear Heart, Ed got pretty lonesome sometimes. Lynn and Carol practically took him in. He was probably the first one at the table when Carol rang the dinner bell. He'd rather eat at the Lillas' than a fancy restaurant, because the food is prepared with tender love and care.

The Lillas' house is so clean, I feel guilty for a second or two, until the food is ready. Even Carol's pots and pans are spotless. Mine look like garage-sale throwaways. She is equally as talented in the kitchen as her husband is. Her table typically includes so many dishes loaded with glorious food that you just can't eat it all. There's always so much left over, she'll put some in a plastic container for you to take home.

Besides being a paralegal for a top law firm in Norfolk, Carol does a lot of work for her church. When Larry was preparing for his transforming surgery, she petitioned the congregation to pray for him. A Carol Lilla comes along only once in a lifetime. When she believes in something or someone, there is no end to her devotion. She will go to the moon for those she cares for. I know this to be true because I have seen it. She's real and I love her.

Carol is particularly devoted to their son, Patrick. Lucky P.J. is so loved. He was born a winner. He can reach for the stars and his mother will hold the ladder. His father will catch him and put him back if he falls.

. . . .

CHAPTER 55

Come Rain or Come Shine

Somewhere along the line, Ed once again forgot that I was important too. We drifted into murky waters a few years ago. I didn't notice the drift at first. Always in the back of my mind I was thankful for not having to worry about being knocked around and verbally abused. Then I realized that Ed was still a control freak. We argued often. I didn't know what to do.

One day while we were arguing, I said, "Mister, do you know what our problem is? The day we slipped off to North Carolina and were secretly married is our problem. No one knew we were getting married. Nobody was invited, not even God. God isn't in your life; only you are. There's no room for anyone else, and without help from Him, you don't have a prayer. Furthermore, we don't have a prayer. The big thing is control. You are afraid to admit that you are powerless to change your heart or save your own marriage." It was quite a direct approach.

Then I thought I was hearing things. Ed agreed. He asked me for help. He said he was willing to do anything to make things right and good between us. For a moment I wondered if he was blowing smoke to throw me off. He insisted that he was being truthful. He admitted that he needed divine assistance. I had to think for a moment. Ed had thrown me a nice curve.

Ed said he couldn't handle things alone anymore. All he did was create more problems. Boy, did I know how that felt! He went on to say that if making a commitment to God and turning my life over to Him had helped me, then it could help him too. He wanted to be a good husband and friend; he didn't want to continue hurting me. He was tired and realized that there was something missing in him. He was ready to let God take over the throne in his heart.

I thought about what he had said and wondered what I could do to have a significant impact on Ed. I do have a flair for drama. I decided that a wedding ceremony would be a wonderful new beginning. I picked out a wedding song, and I gave it to my new husband to keep with him always:

> I'm gonna love you like nobody's loved you,
> Come rain or come shine. . . .[1]

God Himself was there by special invitation from my husband and new friend, Ed. Our chapel was our bedroom. We knelt on a blanket on the floor. We held hands by candlelight, and Ed invited the spirit of God into his heart and life. He said he was so sorry for the things he had done. We exchanged vows: "I, Ed, take thee, Billie, to be my wedded wife, to have and to hold from this day forward. . . ." He said that he would walk beside me, not in front of me. We cried and held each other. It had been a long twenty years.

In the days that followed, I suggested that Ed see a psychiatrist for help with his control problem. I went with him a couple of times.

My husband shows some definite signs that Someone else is living inside of him now.

The way I see it, I have maybe twenty good years left. Ed and I are fairly healthy and can enjoy our lives together. That is, if he can see me as a partner and not an employee. Soon enough, I'll be sitting in a corner somewhere talking to plants. I want these years to be filled with joy—and they can be.

CHAPTER 56

A Mongrel in the Neighborhood

There is no new thing under the sun," according to Ecclesiastes 1:9. To put it another way, the more things change, the more they stay the same. Even though I'm living on Better-Than-Ever Street, I'm still the same frizzy-haired girl wandering around in search of love and acceptance. The names of my neighbors have been changed, but they are all caring people and the lessons are the same. Sometimes I travel farther than I had when I was a kid, but I still find that we are all in this world together, and everyone has something to give and a story to tell.

Directly across the street live the Hoffmanns. Sue Hoffmann is a human whirlwind who never sits still. She is president of the Mid-Atlantic African Violet Society and an authority of violets. There are over seven hundred incredibly beautiful plants in her home. If she isn't tending her indoor garden, she's playing string bass in the Virginia Beach Symphony Orchestra. She teaches cello and string bass and plays the piano. Sue and her husband, Norman, have two active children, Lauren and Wyatt. If you are lucky enough to catch her in the yard, she will open herself to you. She has that rare gift of making you feel as if you are the only person in the world at that particular moment. She is beautiful, caring, and gifted, and I love her.

Next to the Hoffmanns live Dr. and Mrs. Andrew McDearmid. Andrew is a retired Bible scholar. Their home is filled with mementos of his missionary travels to India and other countries. Bernice is a gracious hostess who loves to entertain. Their nephew, Kevin, is my granddaughter Elizabeth's boyfriend. I saw him outside one day and thought he would be a nice friend for Elizabeth when she visits us in the summer. I struck up a conversation with him and showed him her picture. They have been seeing each other for over three years. Kevin attends Tidewater Community College and works part-time for a veterinarian.

My friend Virgie Norman lives in a nursing home fifteen minutes away. I met her one day when I was visiting an angel whose name was Annie Basham. Annie said all she wanted in this world was to go home to be with Jesus and her late husband. I know she's happy now. Virgie was Annie's roommate. When she glanced my way, I saw a mischievous little girl dancing in those flashing eyes of hers. Virgie is, and always has been, a country girl, steady as a rock, everyone's mother. Like my sister Diane, Virgie took care of everybody else and never had a childhood. The little girl inside couldn't come out to play because she had too much to do, but she's a very patient girl. She stays there, waiting. When Virgie smiles, I can picture the girl for a moment. She says, "I'm here. I'm still here. I can laugh and I can sing." Virgie Norman is beautiful, just plain good, and I love her.

Right down the hall and to the left is a fine lady, the gentlest kind of well-bred lady, who doesn't know the seamy or crude side of life. She wouldn't even know what it was if it were staring her right in the face. Helen is ninety-six now. She can still lose herself in a story of unrequited love and weep. Helen Harris was the only daughter of a prominent physician. She was educated and well traveled. Helen does more good, lying bedridden, than some folks do in their entire lives. She is a prayer warrior and considers it a serious occupation. If I have a special need or concern, Helen starts in and gets the job done. Helen is a beautiful person, pure and sweet, and I love her.

My friend Judy Cannon loves me all the way from Bracey, Virginia. She's a nurse who works at a nearby hospital not far from our summer home. Judy is carrying on the work of her late husband, Morris. He left us a legacy of love in his music. She sings gospel songs and is the drummer with the Virginia Laymen. They travel all over Virginia warming hearts and reaching out with their very special ministry. Judy is a picture-toting, bragging grandmother. She really has something to brag about. I know because I have met two of her grandchildren, Tucker and Morgan. Anyone can see God in Judy's countenance. She is beautiful, filled with joy, and I love her.

The next friend I want to tell you about is my little girl friend, Karen. Karen is just a few years younger than I am, and she brings out my inner child. I hope she never loses the ability to see with the eyes of a young hopeful. She has been renovating the house next door for over six years and still isn't finished. She gets sidetracked. She may decide to hop on a sailing ship for a barefoot cruise. Perhaps you will see her in a balloon, drifting somewhere with the wind. If not, she may turn up on a safari in Africa. She could be by the side of the road, picking a wildflower for her memory book. You could even find her in a dumpster. More importantly, she will drop everything to come to the aid of a friend. Karen is a true free spirit, beautiful, and I love her.

Karen called me one day to tell me that our neighbors were throwing away some fantastic stuff. Would I like to join her and raid their garbage can? Just when we had the can opened and ready to dive in, up drives Dr. Katherine Law and her real estate broker husband, Mark Holbrook. We were caught red-handed. Any statement from our lips would have been a lame excuse at best, so we just stood there like children caught with our hands in the cookie jar—or garbage can. They took the invasion in stride and, lucky for us, didn't call the police.

Katherine even warmed up and told us that she recently had a near-death experience that changed her life after complications of gall bladder surgery. After she saw the light and went through the tunnel, she saw her mother and father who had recently passed away.

I considered her parents my friends. Rosa herself had two near-death experiences and shared them both with me. Frank was a retired navy captain. He only lived a year after Rosa went to heaven, he missed her so much. He would follow her anywhere she lead him.

Katherine said she saw them clearly. Rosa and Frank shook their heads and told her that she had two children to raise. It was not her time to leave the earth and join them.

My friend of twenty-five years, Nora Wootton, is a great cheerleader. After my son Larry had his transforming surgery, I was so filled with emotions that I had to let it out or explode. I wrote down my feelings and it read like a short story. I was amazed. Then I thought, *Maybe there's somebody out there who is discouraged and needs to know that God is very real and just a prayer away.*

Nora had been praying for Larry, so I visited with her, to share Larry's good news. She's the kind of friend who you know will be there for you, whether you see each other once or twice a year or not. She owns Nora's Quality Consignment Shop. I really enjoy going to see her. When she says, "Hi, Billie," I feel a sense of belonging. She has some great stuff in her store. Everything looks brand new and smells good too. I have a coat fetish, which could cost a fortune if it weren't for Nora. I can buy a coat for less than fifty bucks, and you can't tell it didn't come from some high-class department store and cost three hundred dollars or more.

Anyway, Nora read my Larry story and cried. She said I should do more writing because it was so easy to understand. She pumped me up so much that I sat right down as soon as I got home and decided to let it all hang out. That's what I'm doing for sure. Some folks might never speak to me again, but if one person will read my story and find hope to carry on, then it was all worth it. I'm getting feedback that tells me that something beyond my capability is taking shape here. My friend Nora is an angel of encouragement, and I love her.

Well, that's the way my life story reads so far. Incredible, isn't it? Sometimes I can't wait to get up in the morning to see what's going to happen next. When I think about what might have happened to me, I close my eyes and thank God.

In our attic is a reminder of where I came from. I have kept my daddy's old footlocker that once contained all my earthly possessions. It measures approximately eighteen inches in height and width and thirty inches in length. Today, it would hold neither my spaghetti sauce nor the olives. I can remember what it was like not knowing when I would even have a next meal.

I never dreamed that I would have so much, but this is not the sum of my worth, nor would I want it to be. Things never measure the success or failure of a human life. God put something of value in me that goes beyond material wealth. The beauty of my children and grandchildren alone say that my existence was worthwhile. God kept His eye on us all.

When I tell people this incredible story, some of them find it hard to believe. How I survived through it all is a miracle, and there's no other explanation. Only God could have brought me to the place where I am today. Without His hand guiding me, I shudder to think what the outcome of my life might have been.

The point is this: If God can do it for someone like me, He can do it for anyone. I am a living testimony of God's amazing power and grace. I plan to tell everyone who will listen that there is hope—just look at me.

What are the odds that a fifteen-year-old runaway would even get a high school diploma in the days when disadvantaged women had little or no power? How many teen mothers of the sixties survived to accomplish anything?

Today, I live in an area surrounded by doctors and professional people who know what they are doing. I just appear to know what's going on. I slipped in through the cracks. My home could be pictured in *Better Homes and Gardens*. The summer home that Ed and I built is better than most of the homes I lived in during my lifetime. I'm driving around in a big, black Mercedes Benz—me, little Billie from Norfolk. I don't know what all these pedigreed folks are going to do when they find out they have a mongrel living right in their neighborhood!

I never really did anything great—never went to fine schools, and I surely don't have any family listed in "Who's Who." My IQ is average, nothing special. I did work hard all my life, but lots of people work hard and never get anywhere. What's the answer? How did I end up here and not somewhere else? My path could have lead to addiction, prostitution, or mental illness. Three of the four children I had before I was twenty-one could have ended up as wards of the state. Who do you suppose held me together through trade school with six children at home? The barbershops I owned were successful businesses, and I went on to college. What mortal could accomplish all that without divine intercession?

After reading a few chapters of my life, anyone can see that my judgment was even lacking plain good sense at times. I jumped into impossible situations, wearing rose-colored glasses, and didn't stop to think what the results might be. If left to myself, I would be that same quivering ort of yesterday, always searching for a way out. I didn't come this far on my own power. God let me find out that my father is God Himself. Then He revealed the truth to me that His Son is my only Savior.

Some people never get the message of God's amazing love. They wander around in the wilderness all their lives. The fact is, I accepted the gift of unmerited grace, and by that act of faith, God called me His child. It's all so simple. I was fooled into thinking that the process had to be more complicated and that I wasn't worthy.

When I get to heaven, if Jesus asks me why I think I have a right to enter the pearly gates, I know just what to say. I'll say, "I didn't do one single thing to earn the right to be here. I'm here because I trusted you." Then I'll probably pass out. From what I have read, being in the company of God has that effect on a human. Anyway, that's all I have to give as my reason, and I am convinced that it is enough to get me in the door. After that, I'll find somebody who knows what's happening.

I'm hoping there won't be a long orientation process, because I am looking forward to seeing my son Michael. I hope I don't have to wait long for the marriage supper, either. But I know I'll never be hungry in heaven.

Growing up was something else, but I think I am better off than most people are. At this point, I can handle things with some degree of dignity. I certainly don't worry about things I can't change. It came to pass, that's what I tell myself. Thank God, it didn't come to stay! I wish I had known that years ago; maybe I would have spared myself a lot of grief on my journey.

But God promised in His Word that He would never leave me or forsake me, and I believed it.

My golden friend, Caroline, wouldn't let me forget. Sweet Caroline is my guardian angel here on earth. Her arms reach straight up to His throne and extend down here to me. She held on to my hand for over thirty years. She said she would never let go. She said God loved me and she loved me. I'm still here and hanging on to her hand. Divine love in action.

> I can fly higher than an eagle,
> But you were the wind beneath my wings.[1]

I think of her every time I hear the words.

Epilogue

The last chapter of my life is far from finished. I don't think I am close enough to the edge to write my entire life story! I'm just getting warmed up. For me, the best is yet to be.

Ed and I are still very much in the midst of challenges within ourselves and in our marriage, even after twenty-plus years. But God is still in charge, and I cling to Him for daily direction. I know, boy do I know, that He can do anything.

One evening at prayer, I was nearly to the point of desperation with some things I was grappling with at the time. The still small voice said, "I have given you everything you need to take care of yourself. Now you must use those gifts to help others, and in helping others, you will in fact be helping yourself."

It was then that I wrote the story of my son Larry's transforming surgery.

God never promised that my life would be bliss, but He did promise in His Word that He would be with me through whatever trials I have to face. There's great comfort in trusting that promise.

Most every month now I have a speaking invitation at one of our local churches. I can't tell you how happy that makes me. Deep in my heart of hearts, I know it is my purpose in life. If my life story won't give some people the courage to go on, then whose will? I wish there could have been some other way for me to learn certain lessons, but I don't regret my life and wouldn't change much. Every experience has brought me to who I am today.

I am not bitter, and I never want to be. Nor do I seek revenge on anyone by returning evil for evil. I won't do that. Actually, I feel very blessed to be able to do the things that I do and to have true friends. You can be lonely in a crowd or happy wherever you find yourself. It's really a matter of choice, as most things are in life.

For the first time in my life I'm free! Free to follow my own path. I feel sorry for that woman I once was—the woman who allowed others to control her, who had no real life of her own. I'm not that same woman anymore. I'm stronger and filled with hope. I have a purpose. I don't worry about what other people think or how they live their lives. It isn't up to me to judge. I don't have that right, only God does. One of the greatest lessons I've learned has been, if the people around you don't make you feel good about yourself, then find some people who do and wish the rest the very best.

In spite of everything, my future looks promising and exciting. God is so wonderful. I'm not sure of what the future holds, but I know He knows. And that's good enough for me.

Endnotes

Chapter 3:

1. *It Is No Secret*, (Copyright, 1950: Music Corporation of America,1555 Broadway, 8th Floor, New York, NY 10019-3743; 212-841-8000).

Chapter 5:

1. *Carolina in the Morning*, (Copyright, 1922: Jerome H. Remick & Co.).

Chapter 10:

1. *Little Man, You've Had a Busy Day*, Mabel Wayne, Al Hoffman and Maurice Sigler.

Chapter 11:

1. *In the Summertime,* Ray Dorset, (Copyright: ATV Music Corp., 1970).
2. *Young Love*, (Copyright, 1956: Lowery Music Co., PO Box 9687, Atlanta, GA).

Chapter 35:

1. Grandmama's song, *It Is No Secret* (Copyright, 1950: Music Corporation of America,1555 Broadway, 8th Floor, New York, NY 10019-3743; 212-841-8000).

Chapter 38:
1. *Alice Blue Gown*, (Copyright, 1920: Leo Feist, Inc.).

Chapter 48:
1. *Sweet Caroline,* Lyrics by Neil Diamond, (Copyright, 1969: Stonebridge Music, Los Angeles, CA).

Chapter 51:
1. *You're the Best Thing that Ever Happened to Me*, author unknown.

Chapter 52:
1. *Can't Take My Eyes Off Of You*, (Copyright, 1967: Windswept Pacific and Seasons Four Music Corp.).

Chapter 55:
1. *Come Rain or Come Shine*, (Copyright, 1946: A-M Music Corporation. Rights held by Warner/Chappell Music, Inc., 1290 Avenue of the Americas, New York, NY 10019; 212-399-6910).

Chapter 56:
1. *The Wind Beneath My Wings*, (Copyright 1982, 1983: Warner House of Music & WB Gold Music Corp. c/o Time-Warner, 3300 Warner Boulevard, Burbank, CA 91505-4694).

To order additional copies of

MORE THAN ONE
ANGEL

Call (800)917-BOOK

or send $15.99 plus shipping and handling to

Books Etc.
P.O. Box 4888
Seattle, WA 98104